Retire Reset Recharge

Subrata Mazumder

Published by Subrata Mazumder, 2023.

While every precaution has been taken in the preparation of this book, the publisher assumes no responsibility for errors or omissions, or for damages resulting from the use of the information contained herein.

RETIRE RESET RECHARGE

First edition. May 25, 2023.

ISBN: 979-8215987810

Written by Subrata Mazumder.

Dedicated to my wife

Chapter 1: Introduction to Retirement Planning

The "Retire Reset Recharge" offers practical advice and guidance on retirement planning, covering financial and social aspects. It is written in an easy-to-understand manner and includes real-life examples and resources for further research. This is not a quick-fix book; the author aims to help readers make informed decisions about their retirement by sharing their experiences and giving a roadmap. The book is suitable for anyone considering retirement and targets the average person who dreams of retiring but needs to know the roadmap. The author hopes to help others navigate retirement with ease and confidence.

Retirement-a chapter in a life filled with both excitement and uncertainty. Many wonder, "How much do I need to retire?" In the words of John Doe, "They say only millionaires can retire, but that's not true. Anyone can retire; it's just that some of us may have to work until we're a million years old to afford it!" This humorous remark reflects the misconception that retirement is solely about amassing a fortune. However, there's more to it than meets the eye.

In early 2023, Schroders, a global financial firm, surveyed US retirees to estimate their retirement needs; the average figure was $1.1 million. While this benchmark often takes center stage in finance and public opinion media, experts caution against fixating on this one number. Overemphasizing the pursuit of a million dollars can lead us astray from other crucial aspects of retirement planning and result in unintended consequences.

According to Colin Exelby, CFP, founder of Celestial Wealth Management, using a million dollars as a reference point may be helpful for explanation purposes. Still, it's not a universally applicable solution. Failing to reach this arbitrary goal can cause unnecessary stress and worry. Schroders' 2023 U.S. Retirement Survey revealed that more than half of working adults aged forty-five and older fear that financial pressure could adversely affect their health in retirement. The survey also found that many individuals anticipate falling short of the perceived million-dollar requirement, with one-third not expecting to have saved $250,000 and three-fifths expecting less than $500,000 in savings.

Actual savings data from the Federal Reserve's Survey of Consumer Finances 2019 align with these expectations. Americans aged 45 to 54 had saved an average of $255,000 for retirement, while those aged 55 to 64 had saved an average of $408,000. The aspirations of older Americans are closer to their actual savings, dispelling the notion of a magic number.

Ron Dedesko, a chartered financial analyst and investment consultant, emphasizes that a magic number doesn't exist. While round numbers may hold appeal, it's essential to consider how and where you envision your retirement lifestyle. The cost of living in your desired retirement location, anticipated activities, healthcare expenses, and the possibility of long-term care all factor into your unique retirement needs.

Healthcare costs, in particular, can be a significant expenditure in retirement. Fidelity's calculations indicate that a married couple aged 65 in 2022 will need an average savings of $315,000 after taxes to cover healthcare expenses throughout retirement. However, chronic health concerns may require even more substantial savings.

Additionally, it's crucial to consider the possibility of longevity and the potential need for long-term care. Long-term care insurance can help cover the costs, but it may be prohibitively expensive for many individuals. As the saying goes, "Location is critical." A recent study by LendingTree revealed a wide range of retirement savings requirements across different metropolitan regions in the United States, reflecting the significant influence of regional cost disparities.

While financial considerations are essential, retirement planning extends beyond monetary figures. Danny Lee, a wealth consultant, emphasizes that retirement shouldn't be reduced to a single number. Instead, it's essential to evaluate your unique circumstances, such as marital status, potential inheritances, dependents, and additional sources of income like Social Security or pensions.

" Retire Reset Recharge " is your trusted companion throughout your retirement journey, providing practical tips and real-life stories to help you maximize this exciting new phase of life. From maintaining your physical and mental well-being to building new connections and exploring new passions, this comprehensive resource equips you with the tools to conf to design your dream retirement confidently; retirement is not just a destination; it's a transformative journey filled with opportunities for personal growth, self-care, and fulfillment. Don't wait any longer; let " Retire Reset Recharge " guide you as you embark on this incredible adventure. It is written in an easy-to-understand manner and includes real-life examples and resources for further research. This is not a quick-fix book; the author aims to help readers make informed decisions about their retirement by sharing their experiences and giving a roadmap. The book is suitable for anyone considering retirement and targets the average person who dreams of retiring but needs to know the roadmap. The author hopes to help others navigate retirement with ease and confidence.

Subchapter 1.1: The Importance of Retirement Planning

Regardless of age or current financial situation, retirement planning is essential for everyone. It's like building a solid foundation for your future. Imagine retirement as a new chapter in your life, where you can enjoy the fruits of your labor and pursue your passions without the burden of work.

One of the main reasons retirement planning is crucial is that it helps you ensure financial stability during your golden years. By planning, you can determine how much money you'll need to maintain your desired lifestyle and make the necessary arrangements to achieve those goals. Plus, the earlier you start, the more time your money has to grow through the power of compounding interest.

Many people need clarification about retirement which can hinder their planning efforts. It's important to debunk these myths and set the record straight. For example, you may need more than just Social Security to cover all your expenses. Exploring other sources of income and savings is essential to supplement your retirement funds.

Subchapter 1.2: Common Misconceptions and Challenges

Retirement planning comes with its fair share of misconceptions and challenges that can trip you up if you need to be aware of them. Let's address a few of them here.

First, some believe retirement is too far away to start planning. But time flies; the sooner you begin, the better off you'll be. Creating early allows your investments to grow over an extended period, giving you a significant advantage in building your nest egg.

Another misconception is underestimating your expenses in retirement. It's crucial to account for all potential costs, including healthcare, housing, leisure activities, and unexpected emergencies. A realistic estimate ensures that your savings and income comfortably cover your needs.

One of the challenges we face today is the increasing life expectancy. While it's great that people are living longer, it also means that retirement funds must last longer. This calls for careful planning and consideration of healthcare costs, inflation, and potential long-term care needs.

Subchapter 1.3: Overview of the Changing Retirement Landscape

Retirement has evolved significantly over the years, and it's essential to understand how these changes affect your planning. In the past, many employees could rely on traditional pensions provided by their employers. However, nowadays, self-funded retirement accounts like 401(k)s and IRAs have become more prevalent, shifting the responsibility to individuals to save and invest for their retirement.

Economic and societal changes have also impacted retirement planning. Factors such as globalization, market volatility, and changes in healthcare have made it crucial for individuals to be proactive and take charge of their financial future. It's no longer feasible to rely solely on external factors; we must actively manage our retirement savings.

As we enter 2023, staying updated on recent developments and trends that shape retirement planning is essential. This includes understanding new retirement legislation, exploring innovative investment strategies, and staying informed about tools and resources available to help us navigate the retirement landscape effectively.

Here are some websites and valuable resources that can provide further assistance and knowledge in retirement planning:

- Social Security Administration (SSA) - The official website of the SSA offers comprehensive information on Social Security benefits, retirement eligibility, and planning tools. Visit: www.ssa.gov
- U.S. Department of Labor - The Employee Benefits Security Administration (EBSA) provides resources and guidance on retirement plans, including information on pension rights, 401(k) plans, and retirement savings. Visit: www.dol.gov/agencies/ebsa
- Internal Revenue Service (IRS) - The IRS website offers valuable information on retirement savings plans, tax

implications, and retirement distributions. Visit: www.irs.gov/retirement-plans

- AARP - A nonprofit organization dedicated to empowering older Americans, AARP offers a wide range of resources on retirement planning, including calculators, articles, and expert advice. Visit: www.aarp.org/retirement
- Financial Industry Regulatory Authority (FINRA) - FINRA's website features a Retirement Planning section covering investing, retirement savings, and choosing the right financial advisor. Visit: www.finra.org/investors/retirement-planning
- Vanguard - Vanguard is an investment management company that provides educational resources, retirement calculators, and investment tools to help individuals plan for retirement. Visit: investor.vanguard.com/retirement
- Fidelity - Fidelity offers a variety of retirement planning resources, including retirement calculators, investment guidance, and educational articles. Visit: www.fidelity.com/retirement-planning/overview
- Retirement Research Foundation focuses on aging and retirement research, providing access to studies, reports, and publications on retirement planning and older adults' well-being. Visit: www.rrf.org
- National Institute on Retirement Security (NIRS) - NIRS conducts research and reports on retirement security, including retirement income, savings, and policy-related issues. Visit: www.nirsonline.org
- Your employer's retirement plan provider - Many employers offer retirement planning resources and tools through their retirement plan providers. Check your company's retirement plan website or contact the provider for guidance specific to

your plan.

Remember to use these resources as educational tools and consult a financial advisor or retirement planning professional for personalized advice tailored to your circumstances.

Chapter 2: Early Retirement; Pros and Cons

Early retirement is a dream for many individuals who desire to escape the traditional work routine and enjoy their freedom at a younger age. However, it comes with its own set of advantages and challenges. In this chapter, we will explore the pros and cons of early retirement, providing real-world scenarios, advice, tips, and tricks to help you make an informed decision and successfully navigate the early retirement journey.

Subchapter 2.1: The Pros of Early Retirement

Freedom and Flexibility: One of the significant benefits of early retirement is the freedom to live life on your terms. You can pursue hobbies, travel, spend time with family, or engage in new ventures without the constraints of a traditional job.

Improved Health and Well-being: Early retirement can positively affect physical and mental well-being. You can focus on self-care, stress reduction, and overall wellness, leading to a healthier and happier lifestyle.

Pursuit of Passions: Early retirement allows you to explore your passions and interests. Whether starting a new business, engaging in philanthropy, or pursuing creative endeavors, you have more time to dedicate to activities that bring you joy and fulfillment.

Time for Personal Relationships: With early retirement, you can devote more time to nurturing personal relationships. Building stronger connections with family and friends and cultivating new social networks can enhance your overall quality of life.

Real-World Scenario: David had a successful career in finance and decided to retire at 55. He used his newfound freedom to travel the world, volunteer for charitable causes, and spend quality time with his grandchildren.

Tips and Tricks:

Financial Planning: Early retirement requires meticulous financial planning. Assess your current financial situation, determine your retirement goals, and create a budget that accommodates your lifestyle and long-term needs.

Build a Strong Retirement Portfolio: Maximize contributions to retirement accounts and diversify your investments to ensure a stable and sustainable income stream during early retirement.

Consider Health Insurance: Early retirees may face challenges obtaining affordable health insurance. Explore options such as COBRA, private health insurance, or joining a spouse's plan until you are eligible for Medicare.

Create a Structured Routine: Establish a daily routine incorporating purposeful activities, hobbies, and social interactions to maintain a sense of structure and fulfillment during early retirement.

Subchapter 2.2: The Cons of Early Retirement

Financial Considerations: Early retirement means relying on your savings and investment income for extended periods. You may face economic challenges during retirement if you have not saved enough or your investments underperform.

Social and Identity Changes: Leaving the workforce early can result in losing social connections, professional identity, and a sense of purpose. It's essential to plan for new social networks and engage in meaningful activities to avoid feelings of isolation and boredom.

Reduced Social Security Benefits: Your Social Security benefits may be reduced if you retire before retirement. This reduction could impact your overall retirement income and financial security.

Healthcare Costs: Early retirees may face higher healthcare costs since they are not yet eligible for Medicare. The cost of private health insurance or self-funded healthcare can be a significant financial burden.

Real-World Scenario: Rachel decided to retire at 50 to focus on her health and pursue her passion for painting. However, she underestimated the impact of healthcare costs on her retirement budget, which led to financial stress.

Tips and Tricks:

Conduct a Comprehensive Financial Assessment: Determine the financial feasibility of early retirement by evaluating your expenses, potential income sources, and healthcare costs. Consider consulting with a financial advisor to ensure a solid retirement plan.

Maintain Social Connections: Cultivate new social networks and engage in activities that align with your interests. Join clubs, volunteer organizations, or pursue part-time work to stay connected with others and maintain a sense of purpose.

Plan for Healthcare Costs: Research and compare healthcare options, including private insurance plans, to ensure adequate coverage at a manageable cost. Consider establishing a health savings account (HSA) to save on future medical expenses.

Continuously Monitor and Adjust: Review your retirement plan, investment performance, and financial goals regularly. Adjust your strategy as needed to stay on track and overcome challenges that may arise during early retirement.

Conclusion:

Opting for early retirement holds the allure of freedom, flexibility, and the opportunity to pursue passions at a younger age. However, it necessitates careful contemplation and meticulous planning to ensure long-term financial security, social fulfillment, and overall well-being. It is essential to assess your financial situation, construct a robust retirement portfolio, factor in healthcare costs, and actively engage in meaningful activities to maximize your early retirement years. It's crucial to remember that early retirement is a personal decision, and what may work for one individual may not align with another's circumstances. Evaluate the advantages and disadvantages of your unique goals, aspirations, and individual situation. In the subsequent chapter, we will delve into late retirement, exploring the benefits and considerations associated with retiring later in life.

Here are some websites, books, and valuable resources that can provide further assistance and knowledge on the topic of early retirement, including its pros and cons:

Websites:

- Early Retirement Forum (www.early-retirement.org) - An online community where individuals discuss early retirement strategies, share experiences, and provide advice.
- Mr. Money Mustache (www.mrmoneymustache.com) - A popular personal finance blog exploring early retirement, financial independence, and frugal living principles.
- Financial Samurai (www.financialsamurai.com) - A blog that covers a wide range of personal finance topics, including early retirement strategies and financial independence.
- Retire Early (www.retireearlylifestyle.com) - A website dedicated to early retirement, featuring articles, interviews, and resources for those seeking to retire early.

Books:

- "The Simple Path to Wealth: Your Road Map to Financial Independence and a Rich, Free Life" by JL Collins - This book offers insights into achieving financial independence and early retirement through simple investment strategies.

- "How to Retire Early: Your Guide to Getting Rich Slowly and Retiring on Less" by Robert and Robin Charlton - This book provides practical advice on saving, investing, and planning for early retirement.
- "Quit Like a Millionaire: No Gimmicks, Luck, or Trust Fund Required" by Kristy Shen and Bryce Leung - The authors share their journey to early retirement and offer strategies for achieving financial independence.

- "Your Money or Your Life: 9 Steps to Transforming Your Relationship with Money and Achieving Financial Independence" by Vicki Robin and Joe Dominguez - This classic book explores the concept of financial independence and offers practical guidance for achieving it.

Valuable Resources:

- Explore the online community of FIRE (Financial Independence, Retire Early) enthusiasts by joining the Reddit communities of r/financial independence and r/leanfire. These subreddits provide a platform for engaging in discussions, seeking advice, and learning from others actively pursuing early retirement. By joining these communities, you can gain valuable insights, exchange ideas, and connect with like-minded individuals who share similar goals of achieving financial independence and retiring early. Participating in these discussions can offer knowledge, firsthand experiences, and practical tips to help you on your journey towards early retirement; FIRECalc (www.firecalc.com) - A retirement calculator designed for early retirement planning, considering different investment strategies and scenarios.
- Bogleheads (www.bogleheads.org) - An online community focused on low-cost investing and financial planning, where you can find discussions about early retirement.

Remember to approach early retirement carefully and consult a financial advisor or retirement planning professional to assess your situation and goals. These resources can provide valuable insights and perspectives, but personalized advice is essential for making informed decisions.

Chapter 3: Retirement Planning For Couples

Couples should plan for retirement together to ensure that both partners are on the same page regarding their retirement goals and strategies. Couples can pool their resources and leverage their combined savings to maximize their retirement income by working together. Planning for retirement as a team also promotes open communication and helps couples avoid potential conflicts. Furthermore, couples who plan for retirement together are better equipped to manage unexpected events and changes in life circumstances, such as illness or a job loss. Ultimately, couples who plan together have a more substantial chance of achieving their retirement goals and enjoying a financially secure retirement.

Subchapter 3.1: Aligning Retirement Goals as a Couple

It is essential to underline how important it is for couples to communicate with one another openly and honestly. Couples are encouraged to have open and honest conversations about their retirement plans and to search for areas of agreement to better shape their collective retirement objectives. Examples taken from real life can help to demonstrate the process further: Sam and Lisa discovered that Sam dreams of traveling extensively in retirement. At the same time, Lisa envisions a more settled lifestyle close to their grandchildren. They recognized the importance of compromise and open communication. Through regular discussions and active listening, they developed a retirement plan that incorporates both desires. They decided to spend part of the year traveling and the remaining time near their grandchildren, striking a balance that allows them to enjoy the best of both worlds.

Subchapter 3.2: Combining Finances and Creating a Joint Retirement Budget

Combining finances and creating a joint retirement budget is essential to ensure financial stability during retirement. By pooling resources, couples can create a more comprehensive retirement plan while streamlining their finances and reducing the risk of overspending or financial mismanagement. Creating a joint budget that considers all income streams and expenses, including debt and savings goals, can provide a clear picture of the couple's retirement readiness and identify areas of potential improvement. Additionally, working together on retirement planning can help couples avoid disagreements and build a shared path toward their retirement goals. Combining finances and creating a joint retirement budget is vital to building a secure financial future together as a couple.

Real-life examples: Tom and Sarah evaluated their individual savings, investment accounts, and retirement plans. They decided to combine their financial resources to create a comprehensive retirement budget. By openly discussing their economic aspirations and priorities, they allocated funds to cover shared expenses, such as housing, utilities, and healthcare, while setting aside a portion of their budget for individual pursuits.

Chris and Emily planned for Chris to open a small business in retirement, which required initial investment. They carefully reviewed their finances and adjusted their retirement budget to support this venture while maintaining their desired lifestyle. They ensured a balanced approach that accommodated shared responsibilities and personal aspirations by aligning their financial resources with individual goals.

Consider factors such as housing, transportation, healthcare, daily living expenses, travel, and any specific goals or dreams you have for retirement. By estimating your future financial needs, you can set realistic goals and ensure that your retirement savings sufficiently support your desired lifestyle.

Subchapter 3.3: Health Care Planning and Insurance Coverage

Healthcare planning and insurance coverage are crucial for couples, as healthcare expenses can be a significant burden during retirement. It is essential to consider the cost of healthcare when creating a retirement budget, including understanding available insurance coverage, such as Medicare plans and supplemental policies. Couples should also consider how potential health issues impact their retirement savings and plan accordingly. Additionally, advance directives, such as living wills and durable power of attorney documents, should be discussed and created to ensure that each partner's wishes are respected if health issues arise. By addressing healthcare planning and insurance coverage as a team, couples can better prepare for potential health issues and ensure that unexpected medical costs do not deplete their retirement income.

Real-life examples: John and Mary reviewed their medical histories, considered their family health patterns, and consulted financial planners to estimate future healthcare expenses. They factored in insurance premiums, prescription medications, potential long-term care costs, and possible medical procedures to ensure they had a realistic understanding of their healthcare needs in retirement.

Mike and Karen researched Medicare coverage options and compared the benefits of different Medigap plans. They considered factors such as monthly premiums, deductibles, co-pays, and the coverage gap known as the "Medicare Part D donut hole." By carefully assessing their healthcare needs, they made an informed decision about the supplemental policies that would provide adequate coverage and minimize potential out-of-pocket costs in retirement.

Subchapter 3.4: Estate Planning and Legacy Considerations

Joint estate planning and legacy considerations involve deciding how a couple's assets will be distributed after they pass away. By working together to create a comprehensive estate plan, couples can ensure that their wishes are respected and that their assets are distributed according to their preferences. This may include creating wills and trusts, naming beneficiaries for retirement accounts and life insurance policies, and determining how jointly owned assets will be transferred. In addition to addressing financial considerations, couples should discuss any personal or sentimental items they wish to pass down to specific family members or friends. Joint estate planning can provide peace of mind for couples, knowing that their wishes will be fulfilled and their legacy will be preserved.

Real-life examples:

Jack and Diane sought the guidance of an estate planning attorney to update their wills, establish a trust for their children, and ensure a smooth transition of their assets. They also discussed designating powers of attorney for healthcare and financial matters, ensuring their wishes would be fulfilled in case of incapacity.

Bill and Sarah engaged in conversations about their shared values. They decided to establish a charitable foundation using a portion of their retirement funds to support causes they are passionate about. They researched different philanthropic organizations and consulted with financial advisors to understand the best approach for their charitable giving. By incorporating their values into their estate plan, they aimed to leave a lasting legacy that aligns with their beliefs and positively impacts the community.

As couples engage in estate planning and legacy considerations, it's important to emphasize the significance of regularly reviewing and updating their plans as circumstances change. Couples revisit their estate plans periodically, particularly after significant life events such as the birth of children or grandchildren, financial status changes, or personal priorities.

Furthermore, the importance of involving professionals such as attorneys, financial advisors, and tax experts to ensure that the estate plan aligns with legal requirements and maximizes the benefits for both partners. Encourage couples to communicate openly with these professionals and ask questions to gain a clear understanding of the options available to them.

Remember, each couple's retirement planning journey is unique. These expanded subchapters provide a framework to guide couples through the process. Still, seeking personalized advice and adapting the strategies to specific circumstances and aspirations is essential. By approaching retirement planning as a team, couples can navigate the complexities together and build a solid foundation for a fulfilling and secure future.

Here are some websites, books, and valuable resources that can provide further assistance and knowledge on the topic of retirement planning for couples:

Websites:

- Kiplinger (www.kiplinger.com) - This website offers a dedicated section on retirement planning for couples, covering topics such as joint finances, coordinating retirement dates, and maximizing Social Security benefits.
- Fidelity (www.fidelity.com) - Fidelity provides comprehensive resources on retirement planning for couples, including articles, calculators, and tools to help couples align their retirement goals and manage their finances together.
- Investopedia (www.investopedia.com) - The Retirement Planning section of Investopedia offers information and guidance specifically tailored to couples, addressing topics such as retirement account options, spousal benefits, and

estate planning considerations.

- TIAA (www.tiaa.org) - TIAA's website features a section on retirement planning for couples, offering insights into financial strategies, joint decision-making, and planning for a shared retirement vision.

<u>Books:</u>

- "The Couple's Retirement Puzzle: 10 Must-Have Conversations for Transitioning to the Second Half of Life" by Roberta Taylor and Dorian Mintzer - This book provides practical advice and exercises to help couples navigate the complexities of retirement planning and make informed decisions together.
- "Retire Inspired: It's Not an Age, It's a Financial Number" by Chris Hogan - While not explicitly focused on couples, this book offers guidance on retirement planning, including budgeting, investing, and setting joint financial goals.
- "Retirement for Two: Everything You Need to Know to Thrive Together" by Maryanne Vandervelde - This book explores various aspects of retirement planning for couples, including financial planning, lifestyle considerations, and maintaining a fulfilling relationship in retirement.
- "Smart Couples Finish Rich: 9 Steps to Creating a Rich Future for You and Your Partner" by David Bach - Although not solely focused on retirement, this book provides valuable insights on managing finances, setting joint goals, and planning for a secure financial future.

<u>Valuable Resources:</u>

- Couples Retirement Planning Worksheets - Various financial planning websites offer downloadable worksheets and checklists to help couples navigate retirement planning together. Examples include worksheets for budgeting, retirement savings goals, and evaluating insurance needs.

- Financial Advisors - Seeking guidance from a qualified financial advisor specializing in retirement planning can benefit couples. They can provide personalized advice and help couples create a retirement plan tailored to their circumstantial instances; open communication, shared goals, and joint decision-making are essential to successful retirement planning for couples. These resources can provide valuable insights and guidance, but it's important to adapt them to your unique situation and seek professional advice when necessary.

Chapter 4: Late Retirement: Beneficial Or Not?

Retirement is a significant milestone in life; deciding when to retire can significantly impact your financial, social, and emotional well-being. In recent years, there has been a growing trend of individuals choosing to delay their retirement and continue working beyond the traditional retirement age. This chapter explores the concept of late retirement, examining its potential benefits and drawbacks. From the perspective of someone in retirement or considering retirement, shortly will delve into real-world scenarios, provide advice, and share tips and tricks to help you make an informed decision.

Subchapter 4.1: Financial Considerations and Benefits

Late retirement can have several financial advantages that may appeal to those in retirement or approaching retirement. Here are some key points to consider:

Increased Savings: Continuing to work allows you to accumulate more savings for retirement. Additional years of earning and protection can boost your nest egg, providing a more significant financial cushion for the future.

Social Security Benefits: Delaying your retirement can result in higher Social Security benefits. The longer you wait to claim your benefits, up to a certain age, the more you can receive monthly payments.

Pension and Retirement Plans: Working longer may increase benefits if you have a pension or retirement plan through your employer. Some plans offer higher payouts for those who retire later or continue working beyond a certain age.

Health Insurance: Healthcare costs are a significant concern for retirees. By working longer, you can maintain access to employer-sponsored health insurance, reducing out-of-pocket expenses.

Post-Retirement Healthcare Expenses: Delaying retirement can provide additional time to save for healthcare expenses, such as long-term care insurance or medical emergencies that may arise in later years.

Real-World Scenario: Mary is considering late retirement. She can maximize her savings, increase her Social Security benefits, and ensure adequate healthcare coverage during retirement by continuing to work for a few more years.

Tips and Tricks:

Review your financial situation: Evaluate your savings, investments, and retirement accounts to determine if working longer significantly improves your financial stability.

Consult a financial advisor: Seek guidance from a financial professional who can help you assess the long-term impact of late retirement on your financial goals.

Create a retirement budget: Calculate your anticipated expenses in retirement, including healthcare costs, and determine if working longer would provide a more comfortable financial situation.

Consider part-time or flexible work options: If continuing full-time work is not appealing, explore part-time or flexible work arrangements that can contribute to your finances while allowing for more leisure time.

Subchapter 4.2: Social and Emotional Considerations

While financial benefits are essential, late retirement can also have social and emotional advantages. Let's explore some key points:

Social Connections: Work often provides opportunities for social interaction, camaraderie, and a sense of purpose. Continuing to work allows you to maintain professional relationships, engage with colleagues, and stay connected to a broader community.

Mental Stimulation: Work can provide intellectual challenges, problem-solving opportunities, and continuous learning. By staying engaged in meaningful work, you can keep your mind sharp and maintain a sense of purpose and fulfillment.

Social Status and Identity: For many individuals, their career and professional identity are integral to their sense of self. Late retirement allows you to retain that identity, providing a smoother transition into retirement.

Personal Development: Late retirement can be an opportunity to explore new interests, pursue hobbies, and even embark on a second career. It offers the freedom to pursue passions and personal growth outside the constraints of traditional employment.

Real-World Scenario: John loves his work and finds fulfillment in his professional life. Although he is eligible for retirement, he decides to continue working part-time, allowing him to stay socially connected, intellectually stimulated, and maintain a sense of purpose.

Tips and Tricks:

Assess your social and emotional needs: Reflect on the importance of social connections, intellectual stimulation, and personal fulfillment and consider how late retirement may impact these factors.

Explore volunteer opportunities: If continuing full-time work could be more appealing, consider volunteering in areas that align with your interests or causes you are passionate about.

Pursue lifelong learning: Engage in educational activities, attend workshops, or enroll in courses to stimulate your mind and explore new areas of interest.

Maintain a healthy work-life balance: If you choose to work late into retirement, ensure you balance work and leisure time. Take breaks, practice self-care, and prioritize activities that bring you joy and relaxation.

Subchapter 4.3: Drawbacks and Challenges of Late Retirement

While late retirement can offer numerous benefits, it is essential to consider the potential drawbacks and challenges involved:

Health Concerns: As individuals age, health issues may arise that can impact their ability to continue working. Late retirement may not be feasible for those facing health challenges or requiring a more relaxed pace of life.

Caregiving Responsibilities: Many retirees are in caregiving roles for elderly parents, grandchildren, or other family members. Late retirement may provide the flexibility and time needed to fulfill these responsibilities.

Burnout and Fatigue: Working for an extended period can lead to burnout and fatigue, particularly if the workload and stress levels remain high. Assessing your energy levels and considering if late retirement would provide the necessary rest is crucial.

Personal Goals and Dreams: Late retirement may postpone pursuing personal goals or dreams outside work. Consider if there are specific aspirations you wish to prioritize and how continuing to work may impact their realization.

Real-World Scenario: Sarah had planned to work until a late retirement age, but due to health concerns, she decided to retire earlier than anticipated. Although she would have preferred to continue working, her well-being and quality of life take precedence.

Tips and Tricks:

Prioritize health and well-being: Regularly evaluate your physical and mental health and make retirement decisions prioritizing your overall well-being.

Plan for caregiving responsibilities: Consider how late retirement may impact your ability to fulfill caregiving duties and make arrangements accordingly.

Establish boundaries and manage workload: If continuing to work, set clear boundaries, communicate your needs, and manage your workload effectively to prevent burnout and maintain a healthy work-life balance.

Reflect on personal goals: Take the time to reflect on your goals and dreams outside of work. Assess if late retirement aligns with your aspirations or if adjusting your retirement plans would be more suitable.

Conclusion:

Late retirement can be a viable option for those in retirement or approaching retirement, offering financial benefits, social connections, and personal fulfillment. However, it is essential to carefully consider the economic, social, and emotional factors involved. Assess your finances, consult with professionals, and reflect on your goals and aspirations. By taking a holistic approach to late retirement, you can make an informed decision that aligns with your needs and priorities. Remember, retirement is a journey, and the path to your chosen course is tailored to your unique circumstances and desires. In the next chapter, we will explore the concept of leisure and travel during retirement, providing tips and insights for making the most of your free time.

Here are some websites, books, and valuable resources that can provide further assistance and knowledge on the topic of late retirement:

Websites:

- AARP (www.aarp.org) - AARP offers a wealth of information on retirement planning, including resources specifically focused on late retirement. Their website provides articles, guides, and tools to help individuals understand the benefits and considerations of retiring later in life.

- Social Security Administration (www.ssa.gov) - The official website of the Social Security Administration provides detailed information on Social Security benefits, including how delaying retirement can impact benefit amounts. It offers calculators and guides to help individuals make informed decisions about late retirement.
- The Balance (www.thebalance.com) - The Retirement Planning section of The Balance covers various aspects of late retirement, discussing the pros and cons, financial considerations, and lifestyle factors to consider. They provide informative articles and resources to help individuals navigate the decision-making process.
- Forbes (www.forbes.com) - Forbes features a range of articles on retirement planning, including insights into late retirement. Their website offers expert advice, research, and analysis to help individuals understand the implications of retiring later in life.

Books:

- "Work Optional: Retire Early the Non-Penny-Pinching Way" by Tanja Hester - While not explicitly focused on late retirement, this book provides valuable insights into retirement planning and explores the concept of financial independence. It can help individuals consider different retirement scenarios, including retiring later in life.
- "How to Make Your Money Last: The Indispensable Retirement Guide" by Jane Bryant Quinn - This comprehensive retirement planning book covers various retirement topics, including late retirement considerations. It

offers strategies for maximizing retirement income and making informed decisions about when to retire.

- "Get What's Yours: The Secrets to Maxing Out Your Social Security" by Laurence J. Kotlikoff, Philip Moeller, and Paul Solman - This book focuses explicitly on Social Security benefits and optimizing benefits, including the impact of retiring later and strategies to maximize lifetime income.

<u>Valuable Resources:</u>

- Retirement Calculators - Several financial websites offer retirement calculators that allow individuals to input their financial information and retirement goals to assess the potential impact of late retirement on their savings, Social Security benefits, and overall financial plan. Examples include calculators from Fidelity, Vanguard, and T. Rowe Price.
- Retirement Planning Workshops and Seminars - Local community centers, financial institutions, and retirement organizations often host workshops and seminars on retirement planning. These events can provide valuable information and insights into late retirement considerations and opportunities to ask questions and learn from experts.

Remember, late retirement is a personal decision that depends on several factors, such as financial readiness, health considerations, and personal goals. These resources can provide valuable information and perspectives to help individuals make informed choices about late retirement. It's essential to consider one's unique circumstances and consult with financial professionals when needed.

Chapter 5: Retirement Planning For Women

Retirement planning is a crucial aspect of financial security and requires careful consideration and preparation. However, retirement planning for women comes with unique challenges and concerns. Women often face specific financial hurdles, such as wage gaps, career breaks for caregiving responsibilities, and longer life expectancies. In this chapter, we will delve into the intricacies of retirement planning for women, providing real-world scenarios, advice, tips, and tricks to help navigate this journey.

Subchapter 5.1: Understanding the Gender Retirement Gap

Wage Gap: Women, on average, earn less than men, resulting in lower lifetime earnings and reduced contributions to retirement accounts. This wage gap can significantly impact retirement savings and the ability to generate income during retirement.

Career Breaks: Women often take career breaks to fulfill caregiving responsibilities for children or aging parents. These career breaks can interrupt their earning potential, reduce retirement savings, and limit access to employer-sponsored retirement benefits.

Longer Life Expectancy: Women typically live longer than men, meaning their retirement savings must stretch further. Adequate planning is essential to ensure financial security throughout their longer retirement years.

Social Security: Women may face unique challenges related to Social Security benefits due to lower lifetime earnings and marital status. Understanding the rules and strategies for claiming Social Security can help maximize benefits.

Real-World Scenario: Lisa worked part-time for several years caring for her children. As a result, her retirement savings were significantly lower than her male counterparts, who had continuous full-time employment. Lisa must develop a strategy to bridge the retirement savings gap and secure her financial future.

Tips and Tricks:

Start saving early: The power of compound interest is crucial. Even small contributions to retirement accounts early on can grow significantly over time.

Maximize employer-sponsored plans: Take full advantage of employer-matched contributions to retirement plans. Contribute at least enough to receive the maximum matching funds.

Negotiate for fair pay: Advocate for equal pay and negotiate your salary to ensure you are fairly compensated for your skills and experience.

Explore spousal retirement benefits: If you are married, consider the potential benefits available through your spouse's retirement plans and Social Security.

Subchapter 5.2: Building a Strong Financial Foundation

Financial Education: Women must take an active role in their financial education. Understanding investment options, retirement accounts, and other financial tools can empower women to make informed decisions.

Emergency Fund: Building an emergency fund is crucial for women to protect themselves from unexpected financial challenges. Aim to set aside three to six months' living expenses in a liquid account.

Retirement Savings: Women should prioritize retirement savings by contributing regularly to retirement accounts such as 401(k)s, IRAs, or other employer-sponsored plans. Aim to save at least 10-15% of your income for retirement.

Diversify Investments: Diversification helps mitigate risk and increase potential returns. Invest in a mix of asset classes, such as stocks, bonds, and real estate, to create a balanced portfolio. Real-World Scenario: Sarah is focused on building a solid financial foundation. She has started attending financial workshops, established an emergency fund, and increased her contributions to her retirement accounts.

Seek financial advice: Consult a financial advisor specializing in retirement planning to create a personalized strategy tailored to your goals and circumstances.

Automate savings: Set up automatic contributions to retirement accounts to ensure consistent savings and avoid the temptation to spend the funds elsewhere.

Take advantage of catch-up contributions: Once you reach the age of fifty, take advantage of the catch-up contribution option, which allows you to contribute additional funds to your retirement accounts.

Review and adjust regularly: Review your retirement plan, investment performance, and financial goals. Adjust your strategy as needed to stay on track.

Subchapter 5.3: Healthcare and Long-Term Care Considerations

Health Insurance: Healthcare costs can be a significant burden during retirement. Evaluate your healthcare options, including Medicare and supplemental insurance plans, to ensure adequate coverage.

Long-Term Care Insurance: Long-term care expenses can deplete retirement savings quickly. Consider the potential benefits of long-term care insurance to protect your financial well-being.

Estate Planning: Develop an estate plan that includes a will, power of attorney, and healthcare proxy. Ensure your wishes are documented and your assets are distributed according to your preferences.

Real-World Scenario: Susan realizes the importance of healthcare and long-term care planning. She explores Medicare options, compares long-term care insurance policies, and consults an estate planning attorney to establish a comprehensive plan.

Tips and Tricks:

Research Medicare options: Understand the distinct parts of Medicare, including Part A, Part B, and supplemental plans. Compare costs, coverage, and potential out-of-pocket expenses.

Evaluate long-term care insurance: Research various insurance policies and consider the benefits and costs. Start planning early to secure more affordable coverage.

Communicate with family: Discuss your healthcare and long-term care plans with loved ones, ensuring they understand your wishes and can support you if necessary.

Conclusion:

Retirement planning for women requires a thoughtful and proactive approach due to challenges such as wage gaps, career breaks, and longer life expectancies. By understanding the gender retirement gap, building a solid financial foundation, and considering healthcare and long-term care needs, women can confidently navigate their retirement journey. Engage in financial education, seek professional advice, and take control of your financial future. Remember, it's always early enough to start planning for retirement.

Here are some websites, books, and valuable resources that can provide further assistance and knowledge on the topic of retirement planning for women:

Websites:

- Women's Institute for a Secure Retirement (WISER) - WISER (www.wiserwomen.org) is a nonprofit organization helping women understand and navigate complex retirement planning issues. Their website offers resources, publications, and tools specifically designed to address women's unique challenges in retirement.
- National Institute on Retirement Security (NIRS) - NIRS (www.nirsonline.org) is a nonprofit research and education organization focused on retirement security. Their website provides research reports, articles, and resources that examine retirement issues affecting women, including the gender pay gap, longevity risk, and caregiving responsibilities.
- U.S. Department of Labor, Women's Bureau - The Women's Bureau (www.dol.gov/agencies/wb) of the U.S. Department of Labor provides resources and information to promote women's economic security and empowerment. Their website offers guides and fact sheets on retirement planning for women, including information on Social Security, pensions, and saving strategies.

- Ellevest (www.ellevest.com) - Ellevest is an online investment platform that serves women's financial needs. Their website features educational articles, tools, and resources that address topics such as investing, retirement planning, and financial independence for women.

Books:

- "Smart Women Finish Rich: 9 Steps to Achieving Financial Security and Funding Your Dreams" by David Bach - This book provides actionable advice and strategies for women to build wealth, save for retirement, and achieve financial security. It offers insights into retirement planning tailored to women's needs and challenges.

- "Money Confidence: Smart Financial Moves for Women" by Suze Orman - Suze Orman explores various aspects of personal finance, including retirement planning, in this book. It guides managing money, investing, and securing a comfortable retirement.
- "The Single Woman's Guide to Retirement" by Jan Cullinane - This book focuses on retirement planning for single women, addressing the unique considerations and challenges they may face. It offers practical advice, real-life examples, and strategies to help single women prepare for a financially secure retirement.

<u>Valuable Resources:</u>

- Retirement Planning Tools for Women - Several financial websites offer retirement planning tools and calculators designed explicitly for women. These tools help individuals assess retirement readiness, estimate savings needs, and explore investment strategies tailored to women's unique circumstances. Examples include tools from Fidelity, Vanguard, and TIAA.
- Women's Retirement Community and Forums - Online communities and forums dedicated to women's retirement planning can provide a supportive environment to discuss concerns, share experiences, and learn from others. Examples include the Women's Institute for a Secure Retirement (WISER) Forum and the Bogleheads Women and Investing forum.

Remember, retirement planning for women involves considering longer life expectancy, potential income disparities, and caregiving responsibilities. These resources can offer valuable insights, information, and strategies to help women make informed decisions and achieve financial security in retirement. It's essential to customize the advice to one's circumstances and consult with financial professionals when needed.

Chapter 6: Setting Retirement Goals

Retirement is a unique phase of life where you can enjoy the fruits of your labor and pursue your passions. Setting clear goals that align with your aspirations and financial needs is essential to make the most of this period. This chapter explores how to identify your retirement goals and lay the foundation for a fulfilling retirement.

Subchapter 6.1: Determining Your Retirement Lifestyle

Retirement offers you the chance to live life on your terms, but it's essential to determine what that means for you. Take some time to envision your ideal retirement lifestyle. How do you want to spend your days? Do you dream of traveling, pursuing hobbies, volunteering, or starting a new business?

Consider your values, interests, and priorities. Reflect on what brings you joy and fulfillment. This will help you shape your retirement goals and ensure your financial plans align with your desired lifestyle.

Subchapter 6.2: Assessing Your Financial Needs

Understanding your financial needs in retirement is crucial for effective planning. Start by assessing your current expenses and how they might change in retirement. Some costs may decrease, such as commuting expenses or work-related expenses. However, other fees, like healthcare and leisure activities, may increase.

Subchapter 6.3: Identifying Personal Goals and Aspirations

Retirement is a time to pursue your passions, explore new interests, and achieve personal goals. Take some time to reflect on what you hope to accomplish during this phase of life. Do you want to learn a new skill, author a book, spend more time with family, or positively impact your community?

Identifying personal goals and aspirations will give your retirement purpose and meaning. It's not just about financial security; it's about creating a fulfilling and purposeful life. By setting specific goals, you can structure your retirement plans and make the financial arrangements to support them.

Remember, retirement is a journey, and your goals may evolve. It's important to reassess and adjust your goals as circumstances change periodically. Flexibility ensures that your retirement remains fulfilling and aligned with your aspirations.

<u>Here are some valuable resources, including websites, books, and other materials, for "Setting Retirement Goals":</u>

<u>Websites:</u>

- AARP (aarp.org): AARP offers a variety of resources and articles on retirement planning, including setting retirement goals. They provide information on financial planning, healthcare, and lifestyle considerations in retirement.
- Retirement Researcher (retirementresearcher.com): The Retirement Researcher website, created by retirement researcher and author Wade Pfau, offers insights and resources on setting retirement goals, including retirement income planning, portfolio strategies, and managing retirement risks.
- The Balance (thebalance.com): The Balance provides a range of articles and guides on retirement planning, including goal

setting. They cover topics such as determining retirement expenses, calculating retirement savings needs, and creating a retirement savings plan.

Books:

- "The Total Money Makeover: A Proven Plan for Financial Fitness" by Dave Ramsey: While not solely focused on retirement, this book helps readers set financial goals, including retirement goals, and provides actionable steps to achieve them. It covers budgeting, debt reduction, and investing for the future.
- "The Number: A Completely Different Way to Think About the Rest of Your Life!" by Lee Eisenberg: This book explores the concept of the "number," which represents the amount of money needed to achieve one's desired lifestyle in retirement. It helps readers set meaningful goals and plan for their retirement accordingly.
- "Your Retirement Quest: 10 Secrets for Creating and Living a Fulfilling Retirement" by Alan Spector and Keith Lawrence: This book guides readers through setting retirement goals, creating a vision for retirement, and developing a plan to achieve those goals. It addresses financial, personal, and lifestyle considerations.

Valuable Resources:

- Retirement Goal Worksheets: Various websites, including retirementplanningworksheets.com and thebalance.com, offer retirement goal worksheets and templates to help you identify and prioritize your retirement goals. These worksheets prompt you to consider lifestyle aspirations, travel plans, and healthcare needs.

- Retirement Planning Calculators: Online retirement planning calculators, such as those provided by Fidelity, Vanguard, and T. Rowe Price, can assist you in setting realistic retirement goals based on factors such as your desired retirement age, income needs, and expected expenses. These tools provide insights into savings targets and investment strategies to meet your goals.
- Financial Planners or Retirement Coaches: Seeking guidance from a qualified financial planner or retirement coach can be valuable when setting retirement goals. These professionals can help you assess your financial situation, define your goals, and develop a personalized plan.

Remember, setting retirement goals is a personal and individualized process. When determining your retirement goals, you must consider your unique circumstances, lifestyle preferences, and financial objectives. Consulting with financial professionals and utilizing reputable resources can provide valuable insights and assistance.

Chapter 7: Understanding Retirement Accounts

Retirement accounts are crucial in building your nest egg and securing your financial future. In this chapter, we'll dive into the types of retirement accounts available, their features, and how they can help you achieve your retirement goals.

Subchapter 7.1: Overview of Different Retirement Accounts

Retirement accounts come in various forms, each with its rules and benefits. Some common types include 401(k)s, IRAs (Traditional and Roth), and SEP-IRAs. It's essential to understand the basics of each account to determine which ones suit your needs.

A 401(k) is an employer-sponsored retirement plan, while individuals can open IRAs. Traditional IRAs offer potential tax deductions on contributions, while Roth IRAs provide tax-free withdrawals in retirement. SEP-IRAs are designed for self-employed individuals or small business owners. By familiarizing yourself with the different account options, you can make informed decisions about where to invest your money.

Subchapter 7.2: Contributions, Withdrawals, and Tax Implications

Understanding the rules around contributions, withdrawals, and tax implications is essential for maximizing the benefits of your retirement accounts.

Contributions: Retirement accounts have contribution limits, which may vary depending on the type of account and your age. It's essential to be aware of these limits and contribute as much as possible to take advantage of tax advantages and employer-matching contributions.

Withdrawals: Retirement accounts have specific rules regarding when and how to withdraw funds. Some reports have early withdrawal penalties if you take money out before a certain age. Others require you to take minimum distributions (RMDs) once you reach a certain age.

Tax Implications: The tax treatment of retirement accounts varies. Traditional retirement accounts offer tax-deferred growth, meaning you'll pay taxes on withdrawals in retirement. Roth reports, on the other hand, provide tax-free withdrawals. Understanding the tax implications will help you strategize your contributions and withdrawals to minimize taxes and optimize your retirement income.

Subchapter 7.3: Choosing the Right Retirement Account(s) for Your Needs

Choosing the proper retirement account(s) depends on numerous factors, including employment situation, income level, and tax goals. Consider your eligibility for different account types and assess which ones align with your retirement objectives.

Suppose you have access to an employer-sponsored retirement plan like a 401(k), and your employer offers matching contributions. In that case, contributing at least enough to maximize the employer match is often advisable. Consider opening an IRA to supplement your retirement savings and provide additional flexibility.

It's essential to consult with a financial advisor or tax professional to evaluate your options and make informed decisions based on your unique circumstances.

Here are some websites, books, and valuable resources that can provide further assistance and knowledge on the topic of understanding retirement accounts:

Websites:

- Internal Revenue Service (IRS) - The IRS website (www.irs.gov) offers comprehensive information on diverse types of retirement accounts, including 401(k)s, IRAs, and pension plans. It provides detailed guidance on contribution limits, distribution rules, tax implications, and other essential aspects of retirement accounts.

- U.S. Department of Labor - The Department of Labor's website (www.dol.gov) provides resources and publications related to retirement plans, including information on employer-sponsored programs, fiduciary responsibilities, and retirement plan regulations. It offers insights into retirement account options and rules from employee benefits fit perspective.

- Financial Industry Regulatory Authority (FINRA) - FINRA's website (www.finra.org) includes educational materials on retirement accounts and investment topics. Their resources cover retirement planning strategies, understanding several types of retirement accounts, and tips for choosing investments within those accounts.

- Investopedia - Investopedia (www.investopedia.com) is a reliable online resource that provides explanations and articles on various financial topics, including retirement accounts. Their retirement account section covers definitions, rules, and considerations for different retirement plans, helping individuals gain a better understanding.

Books:

- "The Bogleheads' Guide to Retirement Planning" by Taylor Larimore, Mel Lindauer, and Richard A. Ferri - This book offers a comprehensive guide to retirement planning, including detailed explanations of retirement accounts. It provides insights into diverse types of accounts, tax implications, investment strategies, and other vital considerations.

- "Retirement Basics: Help for Broke Baby Boomers" by A.D. Hopkins - Geared towards individuals approaching retirement, this book provides explanations and practical advice on retirement accounts, Social Security, pensions, and other aspects of retirement planning. It offers guidance for making the most of retirement account options.
- "Retirement Savings for Beginners" by Nick Braun - This book is designed for individuals new to retirement planning and provides a beginner-friendly overview of retirement accounts. It covers various retirement plans, contribution limits, tax advantages, and investment strategies to help individuals start their retirement journey.

Valuable Resources:

- Retirement Plan Provider Websites - Many retirement plan providers, such as Vanguard, Fidelity, and Charles Schwab, offer educational resources and tools. These resources provide information on retirement accounts, investment options, retirement calculators, and planning guides specific to the retirement plans they offer.
- Financial Advisors and Planners - Seeking advice from a qualified financial advisor or planner can be invaluable when understanding retirement accounts. They can provide personalized guidance based on individual circumstances and help individuals make informed decisions regarding their retirement savings.

Remember, understanding retirement accounts is crucial for effective retirement planning. These resources can provide valuable insights, explanations, and strategies to help individuals navigate the complexities of retirement accounts, maximize their savings potential, and make informed decisions about their financial future.

Chapter 8: Investment Strategies for Retirement

Investing wisely is crucial for building wealth and achieving your retirement goals. This chapter will explore different investment strategies and considerations to help you make informed decisions about growing your retirement savings.

Subchapter 8.1: Importance of Investment Planning for Retirement

Investment planning is a crucial component of a successful retirement strategy. While saving is important, investing allows your money to grow and potentially outpace inflation. By making intelligent investment decisions, you can maximize the growth of your retirement funds and increase your chances of reaching your goals.

Subchapter 8.2: Diversification and Risk Management

Diversification is a fundamental principle of investment strategy. It involves spreading your investments across different asset classes, such as stocks, bonds, real estate, and other instruments. Diversification helps reduce the risk of significant losses by minimizing exposure to any single investment. Understanding how to create a diversified portfolio that aligns with your risk tolerance and long-term goals is essential.

Risk management is also essential when investing for retirement. As you are near retirement age, it's advisable to gradually shift towards more conservative investments to protect your savings from market volatility. Balancing risk and potential returns is crucial, and it's essential to reassess your portfolio and make adjustments as needed regularly.

Subchapter 8.3: Exploring Different Investment Options

There are various investment options to consider when planning for retirement. Some common choices include stocks, bonds, mutual funds, exchange-traded funds (ETFs), real estate, and annuities. Each option comes with its own set of risks and potential returns.

Stocks offer the potential for long-term growth but also come with market volatility. On the other hand, bonds are considered more conservative investments that provide income and stability. Mutual funds and ETFs offer diversification and professional management, making them popular choices for retirement accounts.

Real estate can be an attractive investment for rental income and potential appreciation, while annuities provide guaranteed income streams for retirement. Evaluating these options is essential based on your risk tolerance, investment horizon, and financial goals.

Subchapter 8.4: Balancing Active and Passive Investing

Regarding investment strategies, you'll encounter active and passive approaches. Active investing involves selecting individual stocks or actively managed funds to outperform the market. Passive investing, on the other hand, focuses on low-cost index funds that aim to replicate the performance of a specific market index.

Both approaches have their merits, and the right balance will depend on your preferences, expertise, and time commitment. Many investors combine both, leveraging passive investments for broad market exposure and using active assets for specific opportunities or sectors they know about.

Here are some websites, books, and valuable resources that can provide further assistance and knowledge on the topic of investment strategies for retirement:

<u>Websites:</u>

- Morningstar (www.morningstar.com) is a reputable financial research and investment management firm. Their website offers a wide range of resources on retirement investment strategies, including articles, analysis, and tools portfolio analyses. They provide insights into asset allocation, diversification, risk management, and fund selection.
- The Balance (www.thebalance.com) is a trusted personal finance and investment advice source. Their retirement section covers various investment strategies suitable for retirement, including target-date funds, index funds, dividend investing, and asset allocation. They provide easy-to-understand explanations and practical guidance.
- Bogleheads (www.bogleheads.org) - The Bogleheads forum is an online community dedicated to the investment philosophy of John C. Bogle, the founder of Vanguard. The website features discussions, resources, and guides on retirement investing, index fund investing, asset allocation, and other related topics. It provides insights from experienced investors.
- Investopedia (www.investopedia.com) - Investopedia is a comprehensive resource for investment education. Their retirement investing section offers articles, tutorials, and guides on investment strategies, retirement account options, risk management, and portfolio construction. It covers both basic and advanced concepts.

<u>Books:</u>

- "The Intelligent Investor" by Benjamin Graham - This classic investment book provides timeless wisdom on value investing and long-term investment strategies. It emphasizes the importance of a disciplined approach to investing and understanding the fundamentals of businesses and markets.

- "The Four Pillars of Investing" by William Bernstein - This book explores the fundamental principles of successful investing and offers guidance on constructing a well-diversified portfolio. It covers topics such as asset allocation, risk management, and the impact of fees on investment returns.

- "Common Sense on Mutual Funds" by John C. Bogle - Written by the founder of Vanguard, this book provides insights into index fund investing and the benefits of low-cost, passive investment strategies. It offers a comprehensive guide to building a portfolio for retirement.

<u>Valuable Resources:</u>

- Financial Advisor - Seeking advice from a qualified financial advisor or planner can be invaluable regarding investment strategies for retirement. They can provide personalized guidance based on individual goals, risk tolerance, and time horizon, helping individuals create an investment plan tailored to their needs.

- Retirement Plan Provider Websites - Many retirement plan providers offer educational resources and tools to help individuals understand and implement investment strategies. These resources often include retirement calculators, investment guides, and model portfolios specific to the retirement plans they offer.

- Financial News and Publications - Staying informed about financial news and market trends can provide valuable insights for retirement investment strategies. Publications like The Wall Street Journal, Bloomberg, and CNBC offer up-to-date information and analysis on markets, investment opportunities, and retirement planning.

Remember, investment strategies for retirement should align with individual goals, risk tolerance, and time horizon. These resources can provide valuable insights, guidance, and tools to help individuals make informed investment decisions, diversify their portfolios, manage risk, and work toward retirement goals.

Chapter 9: Investing in Real Estate: Pros and Cons in Retirement

Retirement is characterized by decreased income, reduced expenses, and the need to maintain a lifestyle without ongoing employment income. Real estate investing is one of the most lucrative and straightforward ways of generating passive income that can sustain the lifestyle people desire in retirement. While the prospect of investing can be exciting, retirees need to know the benefits and drawbacks of real estate investing.

Real estate investment has several benefits for retirees, such as stable and passive income, appreciation, and tax advantages. Real estate investors make money from rent, and the appreciation of their assets over time can lead to significant returns upon their eventual sale. Additionally, real estate investors take advantage of various tax deductions, which can significantly reduce their tax liability. These benefits make investing in real estate appealing to retirees seeking passive income.

However, investing in real estate also comes with risks and potential downsides that require careful consideration. For example, real estate investments can be illiquid, making it challenging to sell the asset quickly in case of unexpected financial setbacks. Such investments may also require significant upfront capital investment, ongoing mortgage loan payments, and property management costs. Additionally, if retirees choose to invest in rental properties, landlord responsibilities may be overwhelming and expensive.

This chapter will discuss the pros and cons of real estate investing in retirement. We will explore the various investment options that retirees can consider, including traditional rental properties, REITs, and crowdfunding platforms. By understanding the potential benefits and risks of investing in real estate, retirees can make informed decisions and tailor their investments to their goals and needs. Achieving financial security and stability in retirement is a crucial goal for many, and investing in real estate can be an important step in achieving that goal.

Subchapter 9.1: Understanding Real Estate Investment

<u>Understanding Real Estate Investment</u>

Real estate investment is the art of putting money into a property to generate profits. Investing in real estate comes in many forms, the most popular being acquiring rental property, flipping real estate, and real estate investment trusts (REITs). Understanding real estate investing requires a comprehensive understanding of the real estate market, knowledge of financing options, and the ability to analyze specific investments' potential risks and returns.

<u>Overview of Real Estate Investment</u>

Real estate investment is a popular way of generating passive income and wealth over the long term. Real estate investments offer several advantages, including stable returns, tax benefits, diversification, and potential appreciation. With the right approach, real estate investors can generate a steady income stream and increase their net worth over time. An overview of real estate investment requires a thorough understanding of different types of properties, financing options, and investment risks. Investing in real estate may not be for everyone, but it can be an exciting and lucrative venture for those who take the time to learn about it. Real estate investment involves purchasing properties to generate income through rental payments or capital appreciation. It is crucial to understand the basics of this investment strategy before exploring its pros and cons.

<u>Types of Real Estate Investments</u>

Various real estate investments are available to potential investors, depending on their interests, resources, and experience. The most popular real estate investments include rental properties, commercial real estate, wholesaling, syndications, and REITs. Rental properties involve buying a residential property and leasing it out to tenants. Commercial real estate is more focused on office and retail properties. At the same time, who the art of finding discounted real estate deals and selling them to other investors at a profit. Syndications represent investment opportunities that require the pooling of the resources to acquire a more significant property and finally allow investors to own real estate without the need to buy or physically manage any properties.

Subchapter 9.2: Pros of Real Estate Investment

<u>Potential for Long-Term Appreciation</u>

Real estate has the potential to appreciate over time, resulting in significant gains for investors. Location, economic growth, and market demand can contribute to property value appreciation.

<u>Steady Cash Flow</u>

Rental properties can provide a steady stream of income through monthly rental payments. This can be particularly beneficial for retirees looking for passive income to supplement their retirement savings.

<u>Tax Benefits</u>

Real estate investors can take advantage of various tax deductions and benefits. Expenses related to property management, maintenance, and mortgage interest payments can be deducted, reducing the overall tax liability.

<u>Inflation Hedge</u>

Real estate is often considered a hedge against inflation. As the cost-of-living increases, rental rates, and property values also tend to rise, allowing investors to maintain their purchasing power.

<u>Portfolio Diversification</u>

Real estate investments allow individuals to diversify their investment portfolio beyond traditional assets like stocks and bonds. Real estate has a different risk-return profile, providing additional verification and potentially reducing overall portfolio volatility.

Subchapter 9.3: Cons of Real Estate Investment

<u>High Initial Investment</u>

Purchasing real estate typically requires a substantial initial investment, including down payments, closing costs, and renovations. This can make it challenging for some individuals to enter the real estate market.

<u>Market Volatility</u>

Real estate markets can experience fluctuations, and property values may decline during economic downturns. Investors should be prepared for market volatility and have a long-term investment horizon to overcome any downturns.

<u>Property Management Responsibilities</u>

Being a real estate investor often involves managing rental properties, addressing maintenance issues, finding tenants, and dealing with various tenant-related matters. These responsibilities can be time-consuming and require active involvement.

<u>Lack of Liquidity</u>

Real estate investments are not liquid compared to other assets like stocks. Selling a property may take time, and there is no guarantee of finding a buyer quickly, especially during market downturns.

<u>Market Dependency</u>

Real estate value is influenced by numerous factors in the local market, such as supply and demand dynamics, economic trends, and demographic characteristics. Investing in real estate necessitates thorough market research and a comprehensive understanding of the dynamics in the market.

Subchapter 9.4: Real-World Scenarios and Tips

Scenario: Mary's Passive Income

Mary, a retiree, is considering investing in a rental property to generate passive income during her retirement. She researches the local rental market, assesses property values, and analyzes rental rates to ensure the investment is financially viable.

<u>Advice</u>: Thorough Market Research

Conduct thorough market research and financial analysis before investing in a rental property. Consider location, rental demand, property condition, and potential rental income. Seek guidance from real estate professionals or property management companies for expert advice.

Scenario: John and Sarah's Limited Capital

John and Sarah are a young, retired couple interested in real estate investment. They have limited capital but want to enter the market. They decide to explore real estate investment trusts (REITs) as a more affordable option that provides exposure to the real estate market.

Advice: Consider REITs

If you have limited capital or prefer a more hands-off approach to real estate investment, consider investing in REITs. REITs are publicly traded companies that own and manage income-generating real estate properties. They offer a way to invest in real estate without direct property ownership.

In conclusion, investing in real estate can provide numerous benefits, including potential long-term appreciation, steady cash flow, tax advantages, inflation protection, and portfolio diversification. However, it is essential to be aware of the challenges, such as high initial investment, market volatility, property management responsibilities, lack of liquidity, and market dependency. By conducting thorough research, seeking professional guidance, and understanding the local market dynamics, individuals can make informed decisions when investing in real estate and increase their chances of success.

Here are some websites, books, and valuable resources that can provide further assistance and knowledge on the topic of investing in real estate, specifically focusing on the pros and cons:

Websites:

- BiggerPockets (www.biggerpockets.com): A comprehensive online community and resource for real estate investors, offering forums, articles, podcasts, and educational materials.
- Investopedia (www.investopedia.com): A financial education website that provides articles, tutorials, and investment guides on assorted topics, including real estate investing.
- National Real Estate Investors Association (www.nationalreia.org): A non-profit organization that supports real estate investors by providing networking opportunities, educational resources, and industry updates.

Books:

- "The Book on Rental Property Investing" by Brandon Turner: This book offers practical advice and strategies for investing in rental properties, covering topics such as property selection, financing, and tenant management.
- "Rich Dad Poor Dad" by Robert Kiyosaki: While not solely focused on real estate, this book introduces investing in assets that generate cash flow and provides valuable insights into financial independence.
- "The Millionaire Real Estate Investor" by Gary Keller: This book explores the strategies and mindset required for successful real estate investing, drawing on the experiences of various successful investors.

Valuable Resources:

- Real estate investment blogs: Websites like www.realestateinvesting.com, www.rentalpreneur.com, and www.fortunebuilders.com/blog offer informative blog posts, case studies, and investment tips.
- Real estate investment podcasts: Podcasts such as "The Real Estate Guys Radio Show," "Real Estate Investing for Cash Flow," and "Real Estate Investing Mastery" provide insights, interviews, and advice from experienced investors.
- Local real estate investment groups and meetups: Joining local investor groups and attending rallies can provide valuable networking opportunities and access to experienced investors who can share their knowledge and experiences.

Always conduct thorough research and due diligence before making investment decisions. Real estate investing involves risks, and you must educate yourself and seek professional advice when necessary.

Chapter 10: Home Safety and Aging in Place

This chapter on "Home Safety and Aging in Place" explores the significance of creating a safe and comfortable living environment for seniors who choose to age in their homes. This chapter delves into various aspects of home safety, including fall prevention, adapting the house to meet changing needs and utilizing technology for enhanced security. It provides real-world scenarios, practical advice, and helpful tips and tricks to assist seniors and their caregivers in establishing a safe and supportive living space.

Subchapter 10.1: Falls Prevention

<u>Understanding the Risk of Falls</u>

Falls are a common concern for seniors, often leading to injuries and a loss of independence. This section highlights the importance of fall prevention and the factors contributing to fall risks, such as poor balance, medication side effects, and hazards in the home.

<u>Creating a Safe Living Environment</u>

This section offers practical tips for creating a safe environment to prevent falls. It includes suggestions for removing trip hazards, improving lighting, installing grab bars and handrails, and using non-slip flooring. Real-world scenarios can be incorporated here to illustrate how these modifications can significantly prevent falls.

<u>Exercises and Balance Training</u>

This section explores various exercise and balance training techniques that seniors can incorporate into their daily routines to improve balance and reduce the risk of falls. It emphasizes the importance of staying active and seeking guidance from healthcare professionals or physical therapists.

Subchapter 10.2: Adapting the Home for Changing Needs

<u>Assessing Current and Future Needs</u>

As individuals age, their needs and abilities may change. This section guides assessing current and future needs to determine necessary home modifications. It covers mobility limitations, accessibility considerations, and the potential need for assistive devices.

<u>Modifying the Living Space</u>

To support aging in place, this section offers practical advice on modifying different areas of the home. It includes tips on adjusting bedroom and bathroom layouts, creating accessible entryways, and optimizing kitchen spaces for convenience and safety. Real-world scenarios can be incorporated to showcase how specific modifications have improved seniors' quality of life.

<u>Seeking Professional Help</u>

When extensive modifications are needed, it is essential to seek professional assistance from contractors, architects, or occupational therapists. This section guides us in finding reputable professionals who are specialized in in-place modifications and highlights the invaluable benefits of their expertise.

Subchapter 10.3: Technology for Added Security

Introduction to Assistive Technology

Advancements in technology have made it easier for seniors to live independently and safely at home. This section introduces several types of assistive technology, such as personal emergency response systems, home monitoring devices, and medication management tools.

Selecting and Using Assistive Technology

To help seniors and their caregivers make informed decisions, this section provides tips on selecting and using assistive technology effectively. It includes considerations like ease of use, compatibility with existing systems, and cost. Real-world scenarios can be incorporated to illustrate how technology has enhanced home safety and peace of mind for seniors.

Staying Connected with Social Technology

This section explores the benefits of social technology for seniors, including video calling platforms, social media, and online communities. It highlights how staying connected digitally can combat social isolation and provide a sense of community and support.

Here are some helpful websites and resources that can provide further assistance and information on home safety and aging in place:

- National Aging in Place Council (NAIPC): The NAIPC is a network of professionals specializing in aging in place. Their website provides resources, articles, and a directory of local experts who can assist with home modifications and aging-in-place planning. Website: https://www.ageinplace.org/
- Home Safety Council: The Home Safety Council offers a variety of resources and information on home safety for seniors. Their website includes safety tips, home safety checklists, and educational materials. Website: https://www.homesafetycouncil.org/
- Eldercare Locator: The Eldercare Locator is a public service provided by the U.S. Administration on Aging. It offers a directory of local services and resources for older adults and their families, including home modification programs and agencies. Website: https://eldercare.acl.gov/
- AARP HomeFit Guide: AARP provides a HomeFit Guide that offers practical tips and recommendations for modifying homes to ensure safety and accessibility. The guide covers preventing falls, improving lighting, and creating accessible bathrooms. Website: https://www.aarp.org/livable-communities/info-2014/aarp-home-fit-guide-aging-in-

place.html
- National Institute on Aging (NIA): The NIA offers a comprehensive guide on fall prevention, including information on risk factors, exercises, and home modifications. Their website also provides resources on various aspects of aging and caregiving. Website: https://www.nia.nih.gov/health/prevent-falls-and-fractures

- Local Aging and Disability Resource Centers (ADRCs): ADRCs provide information and assistance to seniors and individuals with disabilities. They can offer guidance on home safety, home modifications, and available community resources. You can locate your local ADRC online or by contacting your local Area Agency on Aging.
- Occupational Therapists: Consulting with an occupational therapist specializing in home modifications can provide personalized recommendations and solutions based on individual needs. The American Occupational Therapy Association (AOTA) has a directory to help find local occupational therapists. Website: https://www.aota.org/

Always consult with professionals and experts when making significant modifications to your home or considering assistive technology. They can provide personalized guidance and ensure the changes align with your needs and goals for aging in place.

Conclusion:

This chapter concludes by emphasizing the significance of home safety and aging in place. It highlights the importance of fall prevention, adapting the home to changing needs and utilizing technology for added security. By implementing the strategies and tips discussed in this chapter, seniors can create a safe and comfortable living environment supporting their desire to age. Caregivers and family members can also gain valuable insights into ensuring the well-being and independence of their loved ones.

Chapter 11: Reverse Mortgage: When To Take Them

As people age, they often face the challenge of how to finance their retirement years. With limited incomes and rising living costs, ensuring a comfortable standard of living can take time and effort. One option that is becoming increasingly popular is a reverse mortgage. A reverse mortgage is a home loan that allows homeowners aged 62 or older to convert part of their home equity into cash. Reverse mortgages come with unique advantages and disadvantages, making it essential for retirees to know when to take them.

In this chapter, we will explore the ins and outs of reverse mortgages and provide helpful information for retirees considering this option. We will explain how reverse mortgages work, highlight the benefits and drawbacks, and guide readers through deciding whether to take one.

With so much information available, making an informed decision about reverse mortgages can be overwhelming. By breaking down the basics, pointing out the key benefits and risks, and helping readers determine if a reverse mortgage is right for them, we hope to provide clarity and peace of mind. A reverse mortgage can be a potent tool for retirees looking to supplement their retirement income, but it is essential to approach it with caution and knowledge.

Subchapter 11.1: Understanding Reverse Mortgages

A reverse mortgage is a financial product that allows homeowners aged sixty-two and older to convert a portion of their home equity into cash. Unlike traditional mortgages, with a reverse mortgage, the homeowner receives payments from the lender instead of making monthly mortgage payments. The loan is repaid when the homeowner sells the home, moves out, or passes away.

How Reverse Mortgages Work

To qualify for a reverse mortgage, homeowners must meet specific criteria, including age requirements and sufficient home equity. The loan amount is determined based on factors such as the appraised value of the home, the homeowner's age, and current interest rates. The homeowner can receive the loan proceeds in many ways, including a lump sum, monthly payments, a line of credit, or a combination of these options.

Types of Reverse Mortgages

There are three main types of reverse mortgages:

a) Home Equity Conversion Mortgage (HECM): This is the most common type of reverse mortgage insured by the Federal Housing Administration (FHA). It offers various payment options and is subject to specific requirements and regulations.

b) Single-Purpose Reverse Mortgage: These are offered by state and local government agencies or nonprofit organizations and are designed for specific purposes, such as home repairs or property taxes.

c) Proprietary Reverse Mortgage: These are private loans offered by financial institutions and have higher loan limits than HECMs.

Subchapter 11.2: Pros and Cons of Reverse Mortgages

<u>Pros of Reverse Mortgages</u>

Supplement retirement income: Reverse mortgages provide a source of income for retirees, allowing them to cover living expenses or fund desired activities.

No monthly mortgage payments: With a reverse mortgage, homeowners are not required to make monthly payments, reducing financial burdens.

Flexibility in payment options: Borrowers can receive the loan proceeds in several ways, providing flexibility based on their financial needs and goals.

Homeownership retention: As long as homeowners fulfill their obligations, they can remain in the home without the risk of foreclosure.

Cons of Reverse Mortgages

Accrued interest and fees: Reverse mortgages accumulate interest over time, which can significantly reduce the remaining equity in the home. Borrowers should consider the long-term impact on their estate and heirs.

Impact on government benefits: The funds received from a reverse mortgage may affect eligibility for specific government assistance programs, such as Medicaid or Supplemental Security Income (SSI). It's essential to understand the potential consequences before proceeding.

Repayment obligations: Reverse mortgages must be repaid when the homeowner sells the home, moves out, or passes away. This may impact the ability to leave the house to heirs as an inheritance.

Subchapter 11.3: When to Consider a Reverse Mortgage

Financial Stability in Retirement

A reverse mortgage can benefit retirees facing financial challenges or needing additional income to maintain their standard of living. It can supplement retirement savings, cover healthcare expenses, or finance home modifications to age in place.

Paying Off Existing Mortgage or Debts

If homeowners have an existing mortgage or other debts, a reverse mortgage can be used to pay them off, eliminating monthly payments and reducing financial strain.

<u>Delaying Social Security Benefits</u>

Utilizing a reverse mortgage to cover living expenses during the early retirement years can allow homeowners to delay taking Social Security benefits. By employing this strategy, individuals can enhance their future benefit amounts, resulting in more substantial and potentially helpful benefits.

<u>Accessing Home Equity for Investment or Emergency Funds</u>

A reverse mortgage can provide homeowners with a lump sum or line of credit that can be used for investments, emergencies, or unexpected expenses. It can serve as a safety net during times of financial uncertainty.

Subchapter 11.4: Considerations and Tips

Consultation with a Reverse Mortgage Specialist

Before making any decisions, it's crucial to consult with a reverse mortgage specialist who can provide personalized guidance based on individual circumstances. They can explain reverse mortgages' details, benefits, and potential drawbacks.

<u>Understanding the Loan Terms and Costs</u>

Borrowers should thoroughly review and understand the terms and costs of a reverse mortgage. This includes interest rates, fees, and repayment obligations. Comparing different lenders and loan options is essential to make an informed decision.

<u>Exploring Alternatives</u>

Homeowners should consider alternative options before committing to a reverse mortgage. These may include downsizing to a more affordable home, renting, or exploring other financial products designed for <u>retirees.</u>

<u>Financial and Estate Planning</u>

Reverse mortgages are just one piece of the overall retirement and estate planning puzzle. It's essential to consider the long-term financial goals, potential impact on heirs, and general estate planning objectives when evaluating the suitability of a reverse mortgage.

<u>Conclusion</u>

In conclusion, a reverse mortgage can be a valuable financial tool for retirees, providing income, debt relief, and increased financial flexibility. However, it's crucial to carefully consider the pros and cons, consult with experts, and thoroughly understand the terms and costs of reverse mortgages. Each individual's situation is unique, and what may be suitable for one person may not be appropriate for another. By carefully considering and thoroughly researching the decision-making process, retirees can make informed choices that align with their financial goals.

<u>Here are some valuable resources, including websites, books, and other materials, for "Reverse Mortgage: When To Take Them":</u>

<u>Websites:</u>

- National Reverse Mortgage Lenders Association (NRMLA) (nrmla.org): NRMLA is a reputable industry association that provides information and resources on reverse mortgages. Their website offers educational materials, FAQs, and a reverse mortgage calculator to help individuals assess their options.
- U.S. Department of Housing and Urban Development (HUD) (hud.gov): HUD provides comprehensive information on reverse mortgages, including eligibility requirements, loan types, and borrower protections. Their website offers guides, counseling resources, and a reverse mortgage calculator.
- Consumer Financial Protection Bureau (CFPB) (consumerfinance.gov): CFPB provides consumer-focused

information on reverse mortgages. Their website offers guides, videos, and tools to help individuals understand the benefits, risks, and alternatives to reverse mortgages.

<u>Books:</u>

- "Reverse Mortgages For Dummies" by Sarah Glendon Lyons and John E. Lucas: This book provides a comprehensive guide to reverse mortgages, covering eligibility, loan types, costs, and repayment options. It offers insights into when and how to consider a reverse mortgage for retirement planning.
- "Understanding Reverse Mortgages: Increase Your Cash Flow and Minimize Your Stress!" by Sandy Botkin and Tom Dominick: This book provides a detailed overview of reverse mortgages and their potential benefits for retirees. It covers critical considerations, potential pitfalls, and strategies for maximizing the value of a reverse mortgage.

<u>Valuable Resources:</u>

- Reverse Mortgage Counseling Agencies: The U.S. Department of Housing and Urban Development (HUD) provides a list of HUD-approved reverse mortgage counseling agencies. These agencies can provide personalized guidance, explain the intricacies of reverse mortgages, and help individuals make informed decisions.
- Financial Advisors and Mortgage Specialists: Consulting with financial advisors specializing in retirement planning or mortgage specialists experienced in reverse mortgages can offer valuable insights and guidance. These professionals can help assess your financial situation, evaluate the suitability of a reverse mortgage, and provide personalized advice based on your needs and goals.

When considering a reverse mortgage, gathering information from reputable sources, understanding the terms and implications, and considering alternative options are essential. Additionally, exploring multiple resources and consulting with professionals can help you make an informed decision that aligns with your circumstances and financial goals.

Chapter 12: Social Security and Medicare

Social Security and Medicare are two essential programs that play a significant role in retirement planning. In this chapter, we'll explore the ins and outs of Social Security benefits and Medicare coverage, providing you with the knowledge you need to navigate these programs effectively.

Subchapter 12.1: Navigating Social Security Benefits and Eligibility

Social Security is a government program designed to provide a source of income during retirement. Understanding how it works and determining eligibility is crucial for maximizing your benefits. Here's what you need to know:

Eligibility: Most individuals become eligible for Social Security benefits at 62, but the full retirement age (FRA) varies depending on your birth year. Understanding how your chosen retirement age affects the benefits you'll receive is essential.

Benefit Calculation: Social Security benefits are based on your lifetime earnings. The Social Security Administration (SSA) calculates your Average Indexed Monthly Earnings (AIME) and applies a formula to determine your primary insurance amount (PIA). Understanding the benefit calculation process allows you to estimate your future benefits and decide when to start claiming.

Claiming Strategies: You can start claiming Social Security benefits as early as age 62, but your benefits will be reduced. Delaying claiming beyond your FRA can result in higher monthly benefits. When choosing the optimal claiming strategy, consider your financial situation, life expectancy, and retirement goals.

Subchapter 12.2: Understanding Medicare Coverage and Enrollment

Medicare is a federal health insurance program that covers eligible individuals aged sixty-five and older. Understanding the various parts of Medicare and the enrollment process is crucial for accessing healthcare services during retirement. Here's what you need to know:

Medicare Parts: Medicare consists of several parts, including Part A (hospital insurance), Part B (medical insurance), Part C (Medicare Advantage plans), and Part D (prescription drug coverage). Each part covers several aspects of healthcare, and it's essential to understand what is included and any associated costs.

Enrollment Periods: There are specific enrollment periods for Medicare, including the Initial Enrollment Period (IEP), General Enrollment Period (GEP), and Special Enrollment Periods (SEPs). Understanding these enrollment periods is essential to avoid penalties and ensure timely access to coverage.

Supplemental Coverage: Medicare may not cover all of your healthcare expenses. Consider options for additional coverage, such as Medigap policies or Medicare Advantage plans, to fill in any gaps and potentially reduce out-of-pocket costs.

Subchapter 12.3: Maximizing Benefits and Optimizing Healthcare Costs

Maximizing your benefits and optimizing your healthcare costs is essential to make the most of Social Security and Medicare. Here are some strategies to consider:

Timing Social Security: Consider delaying your Social Security benefits to increase monthly payments. If you're still working, evaluate the impact of the earnings limit on your help.

Medicare Coverage Review: Regularly review your Medicare coverage to ensure it meets your healthcare needs. Explore different plans and providers to find the most cost-effective options.

Prescription Drug Plans: Assess your prescription drug needs and compare Medicare Part D plans to find the one that offers the best coverage and affordability for your medications.

Healthcare Savings: Take advantage of healthcare savings accounts, such as Health Savings Accounts (HSAs) or Medical Savings Accounts (MSAs), to save for healthcare expenses and potentially reduce your taxable income.

<u>Here are some websites, books, and valuable resources that can provide further assistance and knowledge on the topics of Social Security and Medicare:</u>
<u>Websites:</u>

- Social Security Administration (www.ssa.gov) - The official website of the Social Security Administration provides comprehensive information on Social Security benefits, retirement planning, eligibility requirements, and application processes. It also offers calculators and tools to estimate benefits and explore different claiming strategies.
- Medicare.gov (www.medicare.gov) - The official U.S. government website for Medicare provides detailed information on Medicare coverage, enrollment, plan options, costs, and preventive services. It offers resources to help individuals understand their Medicare benefits and make informed decisions about healthcare coverage.
- AARP (www.aarp.org) - AARP, a nonprofit organization for older adults, offers a wealth of resources on Social Security, Medicare, and other retirement-related topics. Their website provides articles, guides, interactive tools, and a Q&A section to help individuals navigate the complexities of these

programs.

- Center for Medicare Advocacy (www.medicareadvocacy.org) - The Center for Medicare Advocacy is a nonprofit organization focusing on ensuring access to Medicare and quality healthcare for older adults. Their website offers in-depth information on Medicare policies, coverage issues, and advocacy efforts.

Books:

- "Get What's Yours: The Secrets to Maxing Out Your Social Security" by Laurence J. Kotlikoff, Philip Moeller, and Paul Solman - This book provides valuable insights and strategies for maximizing Social Security benefits. It covers various claiming strategies, spousal benefits, widow/widower benefits, and how to navigate the complexities of the Social Security system.
- "Medicare For Dummies" by Patricia Barry - This book is a comprehensive guide to understanding Medicare coverage, enrollment periods, plan options, and costs. It provides clear explanations and practical advice to help individuals make informed decisions about their healthcare coverage.
- "Social Security, Medicare & Government Pensions" by Joseph Matthews - This book provides a thorough overview of Social Security and Medicare and other government retirement benefits. It covers eligibility requirements, benefit calculations, claiming strategies, and potential pitfalls to be aware of.

Valuable Resources:

- Local Social Security Administration Office - Visiting your local Social Security Administration office can provide personalized assistance and guidance on Social Security benefits, eligibility, and the application process. They can answer specific questions and provide information tailored to your circumstances.

- State Health Insurance Assistance Programs (SHIP) - SHIP programs provide free, unbiased counseling and assistance with Medicare-related matters. They can help individuals understand Medicare coverage options, compare plans, and navigate enrollment. Contact your local SHIP office for personalized service.

- Financial Advisors and Medicare Specialists - Seeking advice from a certified financial advisor or Medicare specialist can be beneficial in understanding the complexities of Social Security and Medicare. They can help individuals optimize their benefits, navigate enrollment, and coordinate healthcare coverage with retirement planning.

Remember, Social Security and Medicare are complex programs, and understanding their rules and benefits is crucial for retirement planning. These resources can provide valuable information, guidance, and tools to help individuals make informed decisions about their Social Security and Medicare options, maximize their benefits, and ensure proper healthcare coverage in retirement.

Chapter 13: Planning for Healthcare Expenses

Planning for healthcare expenses is a crucial aspect of retirement planning. This chapter will explore strategies for estimating healthcare costs, understanding long-term care options, and navigating health insurance considerations.

Subchapter 13.1: Estimating Healthcare Costs in Retirement

Estimating healthcare costs in retirement can help you create a realistic budget and ensure you have adequate funds to cover your medical needs. While it's challenging to predict exact costs, considering the following factors can give you a better understanding:

Medicare Expenses: Understand the various components of Medicare, including premiums, deductibles, copayments, and coinsurance. Research and compare different Medicare plans to determine the one best suit your needs and budget.

Prescription Drugs: Consider the cost of prescription medications you currently take or may require in the future. Evaluate different Medicare Part D plans or explore assistance programs to find affordable options.

Supplemental Coverage: Consider the need for additional health insurance, such as Medigap policies or Medicare Advantage plans, to fill gaps in Medicare coverage and potentially reduce out-of-pocket expenses.

Long-Term Care: Factor in potential long-term care costs, including home care, assisted living, or nursing home care. These expenses can vary significantly depending on your location and the level of care needed.

Subchapter 13.2: Exploring Long-Term Care Options

Planning for long-term care is essential, as it can significantly impact your finances and quality of life in retirement. Consider the following options when exploring long-term care:

Home Care: Determine if staying at home with assistance from home healthcare professionals or family caregivers is viable and affordable. This allows you to age in place while potentially reducing costs associated with facility-based care.

Assisted Living: Research assisted living communities that offer support with daily activities while promoting independence. Assess the costs, services provided, and availability in your desired location.

Nursing Homes: Understand the level of care provided in nursing homes and their associated costs. Consider factors such as location, reputation, and quality of care when evaluating options.

Long-Term Care Insurance: Explore long-term care insurance as a potential means to help cover future long-term care expenses. Assess the policies, premiums, coverage limits, waiting periods, and exclusions to determine if it aligns with your needs and budget.

Subchapter 13.3: Health Insurance Considerations and Strategies

Navigating health insurance is a critical aspect of retirement planning. Consider the following considerations and strategies:

Retiree Health Benefits: Determine if your employer offers retiree health benefits and understand the coverage and costs associated with the plan. Evaluate the need for supplemental coverage alongside Medicare.

Health Savings Accounts (HSAs): If eligible, consider contributing to an HSA to save for future healthcare expenses. HSAs offer tax advantages and can be used to cover eligible medical costs in retirement.

Medigap Policies: Medigap policies, also known as Medicare Supplement Insurance, can help cover expenses that Medicare doesn't fully pay for. Research and compare different Medigap plans to find the one that meets your needs and budget.

Health Insurance Marketplaces: If retiring before age 65 and becoming eligible for Medicare, explore health insurance options available through the Health Insurance Marketplace. Understand the coverage options, subsidies, and enrollment periods.

By considering healthcare costs, exploring long-term care options, and understanding health insurance considerations, you can better plan for healthcare expenses in retirement. This knowledge will help you create a comprehensive retirement budget and make informed decisions about your healthcare needs and financial well-being.

Here are some websites, books, and valuable resources that can provide further assistance and knowledge on planning for healthcare expenses:

Websites:

- Medicare.gov (www.medicare.gov) - The official U.S. government website for Medicare provides comprehensive information on Medicare coverage, enrollment, plan options, costs, and preventive services. It offers resources to help individuals understand their Medicare benefits and make informed decisions about healthcare coverage.
- Healthcare.gov (www.healthcare.gov) - This website provides information on the Health Insurance Marketplace, where individuals can explore and compare health insurance plans. It offers guidance on eligibility, enrollment periods, and subsidies to help make healthcare coverage more affordable.
- AARP (www.aarp.org) - AARP, a nonprofit organization for

older adults, offers resources and information on healthcare planning, Medicare, long-term care, and other health-related topics. Their website provides articles, guides, tools, and a Q&A section to help individuals navigate healthcare choices and costs.

- Centers for Medicare & Medicaid Services (CMS) (www.cms.gov) - The CMS website provides valuable information on Medicare and Medicaid programs, regulations, and coverage options. It offers resources on healthcare costs, quality measures, and access to care.

Books:

- "Medicare For Dummies" by Patricia Barry - This book is a comprehensive guide to understanding Medicare coverage, enrollment periods, plan options, and costs. It provides clear explanations and practical advice to help individuals make informed decisions about their healthcare coverage.
- "The Complete Idiot's Guide to Long-Term Care Planning" by Marilee Driscoll - This book offers insights into planning for long-term care, including understanding options, costs, and strategies to protect assets. It covers long-term care insurance, Medicaid, and other financial planning considerations.
- "The Healthcare Handbook: A Clear and Concise Guide to the United States Healthcare System" by Elisabeth Askin and Nathan Moore - This book provides an overview of the U.S. healthcare system, including insurance options, costs, and resources. It helps readers navigate healthcare decisions and understand how to manage expenses.

Valuable Resources:

- State Health Insurance Assistance Programs (SHIP) - SHIP programs provide free, unbiased counseling and assistance with Medicare-related matters. They can help individuals understand Medicare coverage options, compare plans, and navigate enrollment. Contact your local SHIP office for personalized service.

- Financial Advisors and Certified Health Insurance Professionals - Seeking advice from a certified financial advisor or health insurance professional can be valuable in understanding healthcare expenses and planning. They can help individuals assess their healthcare needs, explore insurance options, and develop strategies to manage healthcare costs in retirement.

- Employer Benefits Office or Human Resources Department - For individuals still employed or approaching retirement, their employer's benefits office or human resources department can provide information on retiree health benefits, continuation options, and other employer-sponsored healthcare resources.

Healthcare expense planning is an essential element of retirement planning. These tools can assist individuals in navigating Medicare, understanding health insurance options, and making informed decisions about healthcare coverage and costs. Consider individual circumstances and engage with professionals to design a comprehensive healthcare plan that meets specific requirements and financial objectives.

Chapter 14: Home Health Care: How To Find And Pay for It

As we age, many of us encounter health challenges that can make living independently difficult. For some, an assisted living facility or nursing home is the answer, but the desire to remain at home is essential for many. Home health care can help meet the needs of seniors who want to age in place while still receiving the support and care they need. The challenge is knowing where to find the right home healthcare services and how to pay for them.

In this write-up, we'll explore the topic of home health care in depth. We'll cover the different types of home health care services available and provide helpful tips for finding the best care providers. We'll also discuss the cost of home health care, including the various payment options available to seniors and their families.

With so many factors to consider, navigating the world of home health care can be an overwhelming experience. By breaking down the essential information and providing practical advice and guidance, we aim to empower seniors and their families to make informed decisions about their healthcare options. Home health care can be a valuable solution for those who wish to maintain their independence and quality of life, and our guide will provide a helpful resource to anyone seeking to explore this option.

Subchapter Chapter 14.1: What is Home Healthcare?

Home healthcare is medical care provided in the patient's home rather than a healthcare facility. It is intended to help individuals who cannot leave their homes due to medical conditions or disabilities. Home healthcare services can include:

1. Skilled nursing care may involve assisting with wound care, injections, medication management, and other medical needs.

2. Physical therapy - Providing exercises and treatments to help individuals regain strength, improve balance, and reduce pain.

3. Occupational therapy - Helping individuals with daily activities such as bathing or dressing.

4. Speech therapy - Helping individuals with speech and swallowing difficulties.

5. Medical social services - Assistance with insurance and community resources.

6. Home health aides - Providing personal care such as bathing, grooming, and feeding.

Subchapter 14.2: How to Find Home Healthcare Services

Finding the right home healthcare services is integral to getting the needed care. Here are some ways to find home healthcare services:

1. Check with the doctor - ask the patient's healthcare provider if they can recommend any home healthcare agencies.

2. Ask friends or family - They may have experience with home healthcare services or know someone who has.

3. Search online – Many directories and resources can provide information about home healthcare agencies in the area.

4. Use a placement agency - Placement agencies specialize in matching caregivers to patients and can assist with finding appropriate home healthcare services.

Subchapter 14.3: Paying for Home Healthcare Services

Home healthcare services can be expensive, and it is essential to understand the costs and how to pay for them. There are several options for paying for home healthcare services, including:

1. Medicare - Medicare will cover home health services for those who meet specific criteria. Medicare typically pays for 100% of the cost of skilled nursing care and up to 80% of other benefits.

2. Medicaid - For those who meet income and asset eligibility requirements, Medicaid can help cover the cost of home healthcare services.

3. Private insurance - Check with the provider to see what types of home healthcare services are covered and how much they will pay.

4. Out of pocket - Paying for home healthcare services may be necessary if insurance does not cover the costs.

Subchapter 14.4: Choosing the Right Home Healthcare Provider

Choosing the right home healthcare provider is essential to ensure the patient receives the best care possible. There are several factors to consider when selecting a home healthcare provider, including:

1. License and accreditation - The provider should be licensed and accredited by the state to provide home healthcare services.

2. Reputation - Look for reviews and references from previous patients or healthcare professionals.

3. Experience - The provider should have experience providing the specific type of care needed.

4. Quality of Care - Look at the provider's record and performance in various quality measures.

5. Cost - Consider the costs of the provider's services and how much insurance will cover.

Here are some websites, books, and valuable resources that can provide further assistance and knowledge on finding and paying for home health care:

Websites:

- Medicare.gov (www.medicare.gov) - The official U.S. government website for Medicare provides information on Medicare coverage, including eligibility, services covered, and how to find and compare Medicare-certified home health agencies.
- Eldercare Locator (www.eldercare.acl.gov) - The Eldercare Locator is a U.S. Administration on Aging public service. It helps individuals and their families locate local resources for home health care, including home health agencies, adult day care centers, and other supportive services.
- Home Care Association of America (www.hcaoa.org) - The Home Care Association of America is a national association representing the industry. Their website offers resources and tools for finding and selecting home care providers and information on home care services and payment options.
- National Association for Home Care & Hospice (www.nahc.org) - The National Association for Home Care & Hospice is a professional organization representing home care and hospice agencies. Their website provides information on home health care, including finding providers, understanding services, and navigating payment options.

Books:

- "How to Care for Aging Parents: A One-Stop Resource for All Your Medical, Financial, Housing, and Emotional Issues" by Virginia Morris - This comprehensive book covers a wide range of topics related to caring for aging parents, including home health care. It offers practical advice, resources, and guidance on finding and paying for home health care services.

- "The Complete Guide to Medicaid and Nursing Home Costs: How to Keep Your Family Assets Protected" by Atlantic Publishing Group - This book focuses on Medicaid planning and covers strategies for protecting assets while accessing Medicaid benefits, which can help cover home health care costs for eligible individuals.
- "The Complete Idiot's Guide to Long-Term Care Planning" by Marilee Driscoll - This book offers practical advice on planning for long-term care, including nursing home costs and strategies to protect family assets. It covers Medicaid planning, long-term care insurance, and legal considerations.
- "Medicaid Secrets: How to Protect Your Family's Assets from Devastating Nursing Home Costs" by K. Gabriel Heiser - While this book focuses on Medicaid, it provides insights into nursing home costs and asset protection strategies. It covers eligibility rules, estate planning techniques, and tips for navigating the Medicaid application process.
- "Nolo's Guide to Social Security Disability: Getting & Keeping Your Benefits" by David A. Morton III and Sandra Buys - Although this book primarily focuses on Social Security Disability benefits, it can help understand government benefits programs and their interactions with Medicare and long-term care.
- Please remember that book availability and titles may differ depending on your area and publishing dates. Before making a purchase, always read the book description, read reviews, and check the author's trustworthiness to ensure it corresponds with your unique requirements and interests. Valuable _Resources:_

- Aging and Disability Resource Centers (ADRCs) - ADRCs are local agencies that provide information and assistance on long-term care options, including home health care. They can help individuals and families navigate finding and paying for home health care services.
- State Medicaid Offices - Each state has a Medicaid program that may provide coverage for home health care services for eligible individuals. Contact your state's Medicaid office for information on eligibility criteria, covered services, and the application process.
- Local Supportive Services Organizations - Local organizations and nonprofits may offer support and resources for finding and paying for home health care. These organizations can guide available services, financial assistance programs, and caregiver support.

Remember, the specific resources and programs available may vary based on your location and individual circumstances. Researching and consulting with local agencies, professionals, and trusted sources is essential to get the most accurate and up-to-date information on finding and paying for home health care. Please note that the availability and titles of books may vary based on your location and publication dates. Reviewing the book's description, reading reviews, and checking the author's credibility before purchasing it aligns with your specific needs and interests is always recommended.

Chapter 15: Assisted Living: How To Choose The Best Facilities

As individuals approach retirement, the question of long-term care and housing options becomes increasingly important. Assisted living facilities offer a supportive and engaging environment for seniors who require some assistance with daily activities while still maintaining their independence. The decision to move to an assisted living facility is significant, and it is crucial to choose the best facility that meets individual needs and preferences.

This chapter aims to provide guidance and insights into selecting the best assisted living facility. We will explore the benefits of assisted living, discuss key considerations when evaluating facilities, and provide tips and strategies for making an informed decision.

It will provide an overview of assisted living and how it differs from other long-term care options. Understanding the concept of assisted living and its benefits will help retirees and their families make a well-informed choice.

Next, we will explore the importance of assessing personal needs and preferences. Every individual has unique requirements regarding care, social engagement, and lifestyle. We will guide readers through a self-assessment process to identify these specific needs and preferences, ensuring that the chosen assisted living facility can adequately meet them.

Once personal needs are identified, evaluating potential facilities becomes crucial. We will discuss essential factors such as location, proximity to loved ones and amenities, facility size and layout, safety measures, and the qualifications and experience of the staff. Considering these factors will enable individuals to narrow their options and focus on facilities that align with their requirements.

Lastly, we will explore the services and amenities offered by assisted living facilities. These can range from assistance with activities of daily living and medication management to social activities, dining options, and transportation services. Understanding the range of services available will allow individuals to choose a facility that provides the necessary support and promotes a fulfilling and engaging lifestyle.

Subchapter 15.1: Understanding Assisted Living

Assisted living facilities are residential communities designed to assist with activities of daily living (ADLs) for older adults who require some support. These facilities offer various services, including help with bathing, dressing, medication management, meals, and housekeeping. Choosing the best-assisted living facility requires careful consideration and research to ensure a comfortable and safe living environment for yourself or your loved one.

Types of Assisted Living Facilities

There are several types of assisted living facilities, including:

a) Independent Living Communities: These communities are suitable for older adults who are still active and can perform most daily tasks independently but prefer the social environment and convenience of living in a community setting.

b) Residential Care Homes: Also known as adult foster homes, these facilities provide care in a smaller, more intimate setting, typically accommodating fewer residents.

c) Continuing Care Retirement Communities (CCRCs): CCRCs offer a continuum of care, providing independent living, assisted living, and skilled nursing care within the same community. Residents can transition to higher levels of care as their needs change.

Subchapter 15.2: Factors to Consider When Choosing an Assisted Living Facility

<u>Location and Accessibility</u>

Consider the facility's location, proximity to family and friends, healthcare services, and amenities like parks, shopping centers, and cultural institutions. Accessibility, including transportation options and proximity to medical facilities, is also essential.

<u>Facility Amenities and Services</u>

Evaluate the amenities and services provided by the facility, such as dining options, recreational activities, fitness centers, libraries, and transportation services. These amenities contribute to the overall quality of life and should align with the individual's interests and preferences.

<u>Staff Qualifications and Ratio</u>

The qualifications and training of the staff are crucial for providing quality care. Inquire about the staff-to-resident ratio to ensure enough caregivers are available to meet the needs of the residents. Ask about staff turnover rates, as consistent and experienced staff can enhance the quality of care.

<u>Licensing and Accreditation</u>

Check if the facility is licensed and accredited by the appropriate regulatory bodies. Licensing ensures that the facility meets specific standards of care and safety. Accreditation from organizations like CARF (Commission on Accreditation of Rehabilitation Facilities) or the Joint Commission can provide additional reassurance of quality.

<u>Social and Recreational Opportunities</u>

Consider the social and recreational opportunities offered by the facility. Engaging activities, outings, and opportunities for social interaction contribute to the overall well-being and happiness of the residents.

<u>Cost and Financial Considerations</u>

Evaluate the cost of the assisted living facility and understand the fee structure. Inquire about what is included in the fees and if there are any additional charges for specific services. Consider the financial implications and explore options such as long-term care insurance, veterans' benefits, or Medicaid waivers that can help cover the costs.

Subchapter 15.3: Touring and Assessing Assisted Living Facilities

<u>Initial Research</u>

Begin by researching and compiling a list of potential assisted living facilities that meet the desired criteria. Utilize online resources, recommendations from healthcare professionals, and feedback from friends and family who may have firsthand experience.

<u>Schedule Facility Visits</u>

Schedule visits to the shortlisted facilities to gain a firsthand impression. Arrange meetings with the facility's staff, including administrators and caregivers, to ask questions and gather information.

<u>Observe the Facility's Environment</u>

During the visit, observe the facility's cleanliness, maintenance, and general ambiance. Please assess the living spaces, communal areas, dining facilities, and outdoor spaces for suitability and appeal.

<u>Interact with Staff and Residents</u>

Engage in conversations with the staff and residents to get a sense of the overall atmosphere and interaction within the community. Ask residents about their experience and satisfaction with the facility's services and support.

<u>Review Contracts and Policies</u>

Carefully review the facility's contracts, policies, and procedures. Pay attention to admission criteria, resident rights, emergency protocols, medication management, and any other specific guidelines that may affect the well-being and comfort of the residents.

Subchapter 15.4: Additional Considerations and Tips

Care Needs Assessment

Before making a final decision, ensuring that the chosen facility can effectively cater to the individual's unique care needs is crucial. It is essential to conduct a comprehensive assessment of the required level of assistance and medical support and verify that the facility has the necessary resources and expertise to provide the care needed.

Reputation and Reviews

Research the facility's reputation by reading online reviews, checking ratings, and seeking feedback from residents and their families. Look for patterns and common themes in the studies to gain insights into the facility's strengths and areas for improvement.

Visit During Different Times

To understand the facility comprehensively, consider visiting at various times of the day and week. This allows for observation of the facility's dynamics, staff availability, and the range of activities and services offered.

Trust Your Gut Feeling

Trust your instincts and intuition when making a decision. Pay attention to how you feel during the visit, the interactions with staff, and the overall atmosphere of the facility. A sense of comfort, safety, and compatibility is essential for a positive assisted living experience.

Conclusion

Choosing the best-assisted living facility is a weighty decision that requires careful consideration of several factors. By understanding the distinct types of facilities, evaluating key considerations, touring and assessing the options, and taking additional tips into account, individuals and their families can make an informed choice that aligns with their needs, preferences, and budget. Finding the right assisted living facility can provide peace of mind, enhanced quality of life, and a supportive environment for aging loved ones.

Here are some valuable resources, websites, and books that can provide further assistance and knowledge on choosing the best-assisted living facilities:

Websites:

- SeniorHomes.com (www.seniorhomes.com) - This website offers a comprehensive directory of assisted living facilities across the United States. It provides detailed information on services, amenities, and user reviews to help you compare and choose the best facility for your needs.

- A Place for Mom (www.aplaceformom.com) - A Place for Mom is a senior living referral service that connects families with various senior care options, including assisted living. Their website provides information on facilities, expert advice, and resources to help you make an informed decision.

- Medicare.gov (www.medicare.gov) - The website of the Centers for Medicare & Medicaid Services (CMS) provides a tool called Nursing Home Compare, which allows you to search and compare assisted living facilities based on quality ratings, health inspections, and staffing information.

- A Place for Mom (www.aplaceformom.com) - A comprehensive online resource that provides information, reviews, and a search tool to help find assisted living facilities based on location and specific needs.

- SeniorAdvisor.com (www.senioradvisor.com) - A website that offers user reviews and ratings of assisted living communities across the United States.

- Assisted Living Federation of America (www.alfa.org) - The website of the largest national association exclusively dedicated to professionally operated assisted living communities. It offers resources, educational materials, and a search tool to find member communities.

- Medicare.gov (www.medicare.gov) - The official website of the U.S. government's Medicare program includes a helpful nursing home compare tool that provides information on the quality of care in Medicare and Medicaid-certified nursing homes.

<u>Books:</u>

- "Assisted Living: Everything You Need to Know to Compassionately Care for Your Elderly Parent" by Vicki Schumacher - This book offers practical guidance on choosing and evaluating assisted living facilities. It covers topics such as understanding contracts, assessing care needs, and ensuring a safe and comfortable environment for your loved one.

- "The Senior Care Organizer: Your Guide to Navigating the Maze of Choices and Managing Senior Care" by Nancy Rowe - While this book covers various aspects of senior care, it includes information on evaluating assisted living facilities. It provides tips on researching options, assessing quality, and making informed decisions.

- "The Assisted Living Residence: A Vision for the Future" by Victor Regnier - This book explores the design and philosophy behind assisted living residences. It discusses the importance of environment and architecture in promoting well-being and provides insights into the evolving models of care in assisted living.

- "How to Find the Best Adult Family Home Care for Your Elderly Parent" by Diane R. Carbo - This book guides selecting the best adult family home care for seniors and offers. It offers advice on evaluating facilities and making informed decisions.

- "Assisted Living: An Insider's View" by Beryl D. Goldman -

Written by a former executive director of an assisted living community, this book supplies insights into the assisted living industry, including facility operations, regulations, and tips for selecting the correct facility.

- "The Complete Eldercare Planner" by Joy Loverde - While not specific to assisted living, this book covers various aspects of eldercare planning, including evaluating care options and making informed decisions about housing, healthcare, and long-term care.

These resources can supply valuable information and guidance for selecting the best assisted living facility for your needs or the needs of your loved ones. It's essential to conduct thorough research, visit facilities in person, and consider individual preferences and requirements when deciding. Please note that the availability and titles of books may vary based on your location and publication dates. Reviewing the book's description, reading reviews, and checking the author's credibility before buying it aligns with your specific needs and interests is always recommended.

Chapter 16: Health: Supporting Physical and Mental Health

Maintaining good health is a crucial aspect of one's retirement years. As the body ages, the risk of developing various health conditions increases. Therefore, retirees must pay particular attention to their health to live a happy and fulfilling life. Eating a balanced diet, engaging in regular physical activity, and getting adequate sleep are all key factors contributing to good health. It's also essential to keep up with regular health check-ups and screenings to detect any health problems early on. A sound social support system can also improve one's overall well-being and support good mental health. Caring for one's health can lead to a more active, enjoyable retirement.

Subchapter 16.1: Physical Health

a. Stay Active: Engage in regular physical activity to support strength, flexibility, and cardiovascular health. Aim for at least 150 minutes of moderate-intensity aerobic activity per week, such as brisk walking, swimming, or cycling. Include strength training exercises at least twice weekly to preserve muscle mass and bone density.

b. Find Enjoyable Exercises: Choose activities that you enjoy and that fit your abilities. To stay motivated and socially engaged, consider joining fitness classes, walking groups, or recreational sports teams.

c. Prioritize Balance and Flexibility: Incorporate exercises that improve balance, such as yoga or tai chi, to reduce the risk of falls. Stretching exercises can enhance flexibility and joint mobility.

d. Keep a Healthy Weight: Eat a well-balanced diet that includes fruits, vegetables, whole grains, lean proteins, and healthy fats. Limit processed foods, sugary snacks, and excessive salt intake. Consult a healthcare professional or a registered dietitian for personalized nutrition guidance.

e. Get Regular Check-ups: Schedule regular health check-ups to check your overall health, manage chronic conditions, and address emerging health concerns. Follow your healthcare provider's screenings, vaccinations, and preventive care recommendations.

Subchapter 16.2: Mental Health:

a. Stay Socially Engaged: Cultivate and keep social connections by joining clubs, volunteer organizations, or community groups. Engage in activities that allow you to interact with others and build meaningful relationships.

b. Pursue Interests and Hobbies: Explore new hobbies, engage in lifelong learning, or participate in creative pursuits. These activities supply mental stimulation, foster personal growth, and boost self-esteem.

c. Practice Mindfulness and Relaxation: Incorporate relaxation techniques into your daily routine, such as meditation, deep breathing exercises, or yoga. These practices can reduce stress, improve mood, and enhance overall well-being.

d. Prioritize Sleep: Aim for 7-9 hours each night. Establish a consistent sleep schedule, create a relaxing bedtime routine, and ensure your sleep environment is comfortable and conducive to restful sleep.

e. Seek Emotional Support: If you experience anxiety, depression, or loneliness, consider seeking professional help from a therapist or counselor. Talk therapy can supply valuable support and strategies for managing emotional well-being.

Subchapter 16.3: Healthy Lifestyle Habits

a. Practice Self-Care: Prioritize self-care activities that promote relaxation, self-reflection, and personal well-being. Engage in activities like reading, listening to music, or spending time in nature.

b. Manage Stress: Implement stress management techniques, such as practicing time management, setting realistic goals, and learning to avoid excessive commitments. Engage in activities that help you unwind, such as taking walks, practicing hobbies, or engaging in creative outlets.

c. Limit Alcohol and Tobacco: If you consume alcohol, do so in moderation. Limit smoking and consider quitting to protect your health and reduce the risk of chronic diseases.

d. Stay mentally active: Engage in activities that challenge your mind, such as puzzles, crosswords, or learning a new language. Continuously seek intellectual stimulation to keep your cognitive abilities sharp.

e. Keep a Positive Outlook: Focus on the positive aspects of retirement, set goals for yourself, and nurture a sense of purpose. Surround yourself with supportive and positive people who uplift and inspire you.

Remember, keeping physical and mental health in retirement is an ongoing process. Regularly reassess your lifestyle habits, adapt to changing needs, and seek professional help when necessary. By prioritizing your well-being, you can enjoy a fulfilling and healthy retirement.

Here are some valuable resources, including websites, and books, which can supply further assistance and knowledge for maintaining physical and mental health:

Websites:

- National Institute on Aging (www.nia.nih.gov) - The official website of the National Institute on Aging offers a wealth of information on healthy aging, exercise, and mental well-being.

- Mayo Clinic Healthy Aging (www.mayoclinic.org/healthy-lifestyle/healthy-aging) - The Mayo Clinic's website is dedicated to healthy aging, providing tips and resources for maintaining physical and mental health as you age.
- SilverSneakers (www.silversneakers.com) - The official website of the SilverSneakers program provides fitness courses, wellness information, and social connections for older individuals through partnering gyms and fitness centers. This program could be offered free of charge by the service provider.

Books:

- "Younger Next Year: Live Strong, Fit, and Sexy - Until You're 80 and Beyond" by Chris Crowley and Henry S. Lodge - This book explores the connection between exercise and aging, providing practical tips and guidance on maintaining physical and mental health as you age.
- "The Aging Brain: Proven Steps to Prevent Dementia and Sharpen Your Mind" by Timothy R. Jennings - This book discusses strategies for maintaining cognitive health and preventing dementia through lifestyle choices, including exercise and other mental health practices.
- "The Blue Zones: Lessons for Living Longer From the People Who've Lived the Longest" by Dan Buettner - While not specific to physical and mental health, this book explores the habits and lifestyles of people in "Blue Zones" around the world, where individuals live exceptionally long and healthy lives.

These resources, including the <u>Silver Sneakers program</u>, can provide valuable information and guidance on maintaining physical and mental health in retirement. Remember to consult healthcare professionals for personalized advice and tailor any exercise or wellness routines to your needs and abilities. These resources can provide valuable information and guidance for selecting the best-assisted living facility for your needs or the needs of your loved ones. It's essential to conduct thorough research, visit facilities in person, and consider individual preferences and requirements when deciding.

Chapter 17: Managing Debt and Expenses

Managing debt and expenses is a crucial aspect of retirement planning. In this chapter, we'll explore strategies for evaluating and reducing debt before retirement, budgeting for retirement expenses, and managing ongoing costs during retirement.

Subchapter 17.1: Evaluating and Reducing Debt Before Retirement

Entering retirement with elevated debt levels can be stressful and strain your finances. Evaluating your current debt situation and developing a plan to reduce and end debt before retiring is essential. Consider the following steps:

Assess Your Debts: List all your outstanding debts, including credit cards, loans, and mortgages. Note each debt's interest rates, repayment terms, and monthly payments.

Prioritize High-Interest Debt: Identify debts with high-interest rates and focus on paying them down first. This may include credit card balances or personal loans. Consider strategies like debt consolidation, refinancing, or negotiating lower interest rates with creditors.

Create a Debt Payoff Plan: Develop a debt payoff plan by allocating extra funds towards debt repayment. Consider using the snowball or avalanche method, where you prioritize paying off debts with the lowest balances or those with the highest interest rates. Choose the approach that works best for you.

Avoid Taking on New Debt: Before retiring, avoid taking on new debt whenever possible. Be mindful of your spending habits and resist the temptation to accumulate more debt. Focus on reducing existing debt to free up more of your retirement income for other expenses.

Subchapter 17.2: Budgeting for Retirement Expenses

Creating a comprehensive retirement budget is essential for managing expenses and ensuring your savings last throughout your retirement year. Follow these steps to develop a realistic budget:

Assess Current Expenses: Begin by evaluating your current expenses. Find essential expenses, such as housing, utilities, healthcare, food, and discretionary expenses, like entertainment, travel, and hobbies. Review your bank statements, bills, and receipts to understand your spending habits accurately.

Estimate Retirement Expenses: Consider how your expenses may change in retirement. For example, you may no longer have work-related expenses like commuting or professional clothing. On the other hand, healthcare costs may increase as you age. Take into account potential inflation and any changes in your lifestyle.

Factor in Income Sources: Consider all potential sources of income in retirement, such as Social Security benefits, pensions, investments, and retirement accounts. Understand how much you can expect to receive from each source and factor that into your budget.

Adjust as Necessary: Continuously evaluate and adjust your budget as needed. Track your expenses and compare them to your budget regularly. If you need to spend more money in certain areas consistently, look for ways to cut back and reallocate funds to align with your priorities.

Subchapter 17.3: Tips for Managing Ongoing Expenses During Retirement

Managing ongoing expenses during retirement is essential for maintaining financial stability. Consider these tips to help you make the most of your retirement income:

Prioritize Essential Expenses: Ensure that your essential expenses, such as housing, healthcare, and basic living costs, are covered first. Make these a priority in your budget and ensure you have sufficient funds.

Explore Cost-Saving Measures: Look for ways to reduce expenses without sacrificing your desired lifestyle. For example, consider downsizing to a smaller home to save on housing costs, find cost-effective leisure activities, or take advantage of senior discounts. Be mindful of your spending habits and seek opportunities to reduce unnecessary expenses.

Review Insurance Coverage: Regularly review your insurance coverage, including health insurance, homeowners or renters insurance, and auto insurance. Assess your needs and shop around to ensure adequate coverage at the best possible rates. Consider adjusting your range as your circumstances change to avoid unnecessary expenses.

Control Discretionary Spending: While enjoying your retirement is essential, be mindful of your discretionary spending. Set a budget for entertainment, travel, and hobbies, and stick to it. Look for affordable or accessible activities in your community, or consider alternative ways to pursue your interests without breaking the bank.

Seek Discounts and Benefits: Take advantage of discounts and benefits available to retirees. Many businesses and organizations offer special senior discounts, dining, and entertainment to travel and shopping. Research local resources and membership programs that provide cost-saving opportunities for retirees.

Stay Financially Informed: Stay informed about your financial situation and regularly review your accounts and investments. Monitor market trends, interest rates, and any retirement income changes. Consider consulting with a financial advisor specializing in retirement planning to ensure you maximize your resources.

You can achieve excellent financial stability and peace of mind by evaluating and reducing debt before retirement, creating a realistic budget, and implementing strategies to manage ongoing expenses. Remember to regularly reassess your financial situation and adjust as needed to stay on track toward your financial goals.

Here are some valuable resources, including websites and books, which can supply further assistance and knowledge for managing debt and expenses in retirement:

Websites:

- AARP (www.aarp.org) - The American Association of Retired Persons (AARP) website provides information and resources on various retirement-related topics, including managing debt and expenses.
- National Council on Aging (www.ncoa.org) - The National Council on Aging offers resources and tools to help older adults manage their finances and make informed decisions about debt and expenses in retirement.
- Consumer Financial Protection Bureau (www.consumerfinance.gov) - The Consumer Financial Protection Bureau provides information and resources to help consumers make informed decisions about managing debt and expenses, including retirement-specific topics.

Books:

- "How to Retire Debt-Free and Wealthy" by Terry R. Hill - This book offers strategies and practical advice for managing debt and building wealth during retirement.
- "The Ultimate Retirement Guide for 50+: Winning Strategies to Make Your Money Last a Lifetime" by Suze Orman - While not solely focused on debt management, this book provides comprehensive guidance on all aspects of

retirement planning, including managing expenses and debt.
- "Retirement for Dummies" by Eric Tyson - This book covers various aspects of retirement planning, including managing debt, budgeting, and controlling expenses.

These publications might provide valuable insights and practical advice on managing debt and retirement spending. Seek competent financial counsel to develop a method tailored to your needs and goals. When deciding, deciding to conduct thorough research, visit facilities in person, and consider individual preferences personalia.

Chapter 18: Travel Planning for Vacation

Retirement is an ideal time to travel and explore novel places without any time restrictions. However, planning for a vacation requires careful consideration of several aspects. In this chapter, we will discuss how to conduct travel planning for holidays in retirement.

Subchapter 18.1: Determine Your Travel Goals

a. Reflect on your interests and preferences: Consider the type of vacation you want to experience. Do you prefer relaxation on a beach, cultural exploration, adventure activities, or a combination of different experiences?

b. Identify your budget: Determine how much you will spend on your vacation, including transportation, accommodation, meals, activities, and additional expenses.

c. Consider your health and mobility: Consider any specific health considerations or limitations that may impact your travel choices.

Subchapter 18.2: Research and Destination Selection

a. Browse travel resources: Explore travel websites, guidebooks, and online forums to gather information about destinations, attractions, and activities.

b. Consider your interests: Identify destinations that align with your goods, whether historical sites, natural landscapes, culinary experiences, or specific cultural events.

c. Assess accessibility and safety: Consider the accessibility of the destination for retirees, including ease of transportation, availability of accommodations with proper facilities, and the overall safety of the location.

Subchapter 18.3: Plan Your Itinerary

a. Decide the duration of your vacation: Decide how long you want to be away and allocate time for travel, exploration, and relaxation.

b. Prioritize experiences: Identify your chosen destination's must-see attractions and activities. Create a list of places you want to visit and experiences you want to have.

c. Allow for flexibility: While planning your itinerary, be mindful of leaving room for relaxation and spontaneous discoveries. Overloading your schedule can be exhausting, so balance planned activities and leisure time.

Subchapter 18.4: Arrange Transportation and Accommodation

a. Book flights or transportation: Research flight options or other modes of transportation that best suit your needs and budget. Consider factors such as direct flights, travel insurance, and flexibility in unforeseen circumstances.

b. Choose accommodations: Decide on the type of accommodation you prefer, whether it's a hotel, vacation rental, bed, breakfast, or resort. Consider factors such as location, amenities, accessibility, and reviews from other travelers.

Subchapter 18.5: Consider Health and Safety

a. Consult your healthcare provider: If you have any pre-existing health conditions, consult your healthcare provider to ensure you are physically fit for travel. Get any necessary vaccinations or medications prescribed for your destination.

b. Purchase travel insurance: Consider buying travel insurance that covers medical emergencies, trip cancellations, and other unforeseen events. Read the policy carefully to understand the coverage and exclusions.

c. Research local customs and regulations: Familiarize yourself with local customs, laws, and safety guidelines for your destination. Be aware of any travel advisories or specific precautions you need to take.

Subchapter 18.6: Pack Smartly and Prepare for the Trip

a. Make a packing list: Create a comprehensive packing list based on the climate and activities you will engage in during your vacation, including clothing, toiletries, medications, travel documents, and electronic devices.

b. Organize important documents: Gather and organize necessary travel documents, including passports, visas, identification cards, travel insurance details, and copies of prescriptions.

c. Inform loved ones: Share your travel plans and itinerary with family or friends, including accommodation contact details and any emergency contacts.

Subchapter 18.7: Enjoy Your Vacation

a. Embrace the experience: Be open to new adventures and cultural backgrounds. Immerse yourself in the local culture, try fresh foods, and engage with the locals.

b. Pace yourself: Take breaks and rest when needed. Listen to your body and adjust your plans to ensure a relaxed and enjoyable vacation.

c. Stay connected to your loved ones: Stay in touch with family and friends while you're away. Share updates, photos, and stories from your trip, and consider scheduling video calls or sending postcards to keep them involved in your experiences.

Subchapter 18.8: Embrace Travel Benefits for

Retirees:

a. Take advantage of senior discounts: Many airlines, hotels, and attractions offer discounted rates for seniors. Research and inquire about available discounts to make your vacation more affordable.

b. Explore off-peak travel: Consider traveling during shoulder seasons or off-peak times to avoid crowds and potentially secure better deals on accommodation and transportation.

c. Use travel rewards and loyalty programs: If you have accumulated travel rewards or belong to loyalty programs, make the most of them to save on flights, accommodations, and other travel-related expenses.

Subchapter 18.9: Stay Safe and Healthy During Your Trip

a. Follow safety guidelines: Adhere to local safety guidelines and regulations, including COVID-19 protocols, to protect yourself and others during your vacation.

b. Practice self-care: Prioritize your well-being by getting enough rest, staying hydrated, and maintaining a healthy diet during your trip. Incorporate relaxation techniques and activities that help you unwind.

c. Stay vigilant: Be aware of your surroundings, secure your belongings, and avoid risky situations. Trust your instincts and take necessary precautions to ensure your safety while traveling.

Subchapter 18.10: Reflect and Cherish the Memories

a. Take time to reflect: Once you return from your vacation, take some time to reflect on the experiences and memories you made. Appreciate the new perspectives gained and the moments of joy and relaxation.

b. Share your experiences: Share your travel stories and photos with others, whether through conversations, social media, or even creating a travel journal or blog. Sharing your experiences can help you relive the memories and inspire others to embark on their adventures.

Travel planning is personal; tailoring it to your preferences and needs is essential. Take the time to plan and prepare for your vacation, but also remain open to spontaneity and unexpected opportunities that may arise along the way. Enjoy the journey and make the most of your well-deserved retirement vacation!

Here are some valuable resources, including websites and books, which can provide further assistance and knowledge for travel planning in retirement:

Websites:

- TripAdvisor (www.tripadvisor.com) - TripAdvisor is a popular travel website that reviews, recommendations, and information on destinations, accommodations, and activities worldwide.
- AARP Travel (www.aarp.org/travel) offers travel resources and discounts tailored to older adults, including destination guides, travel tips, and member benefits.
- Nomadic Matt (www.nomadicmatt.com) - Nomadic Matt is a popular travel blog offering practical tips; Road Scholar (www.roadscholar.org) offers educational travel programs for older adults. They provide many trips, including cultural tours, outdoor adventures, and learning experiences worldwide.
- Travel + Leisure (www.travelandleisure.com) - Travel + Leisure is a popular travel magazine and website that features destination guides, travel tips, and inspiration for all types of travelers, including retirees.
- Senior Travel Expert (www.seniortravelexpert.com) - Senior

Travel Expert is a website that provides travel advice and resources for older adults. It offers destination guides, practical tips, deals, and budget travel advice for retirees and seniors.

<u>Books:</u>

- "The World's Best Retirement Destinations" by Ron Stack - This book provides insights and recommendations for retirees exploring travel destinations worldwide, including information on the cost of living, healthcare, and cultural experiences.
- "Retire Inspired: It's Not an Age, It's a Financial Number" by Chris Hogan - Although not solely focused on travel planning, this book guides achieving financial independence in retirement, which can help fund your travel goals.
- "How to Retire Happy, Wild, and Free: Retirement Wisdom That You Won't Get from Your Financial Advisor" by Ernie J. Zelinski - This book offers a holistic perspective on retirement, including advice on pursuing hobbies, leisure activities, and travel experiences.
- "Retirement on a Shoestring" by Anna Leider - This book offers practical tips and strategies for retirees to travel on a budget, including information on finding affordable accommodations, transportation, and activities.
- "The Bucket List: 1000 Adventures Big & Small" by Kath Stathers - Although not focused solely on retirement, this book provides a comprehensive list of travel experiences and adventures around the world, inspiring retirees to create their travel bucket list.

These extra resources can further help you plan and enjoy your retirement travels, whether you are seeking options that are friendly to your financial situation, educational experiences, or inspiration for your travel bucket list. When organizing your trip excursions, consider your particular tastes, hobbies, and any health requirements you may have.

Chapter 19: Downsizing/ Decluttering

Subchapter 19.1: Downsizing

As people retire, many downsize their homes and simplify their lives. Downsizing can bring many benefits, including reduced expenses, less maintenance, and fewer responsibilities. However, the process of downsizing can also be overwhelming and stressful. Here are some tips for making downsizing in retirement a positive experience.

1. Start Early: Begin the downsizing process several months or even years before retirement. This will give you ample time to sort through your belongings, sell or donate items, and find a smaller home that fits your needs and budget.

2. Think About Your Future Needs: Consider your future needs when choosing a smaller home. This includes accessibility, convenience, and proximity to friends and family. You should also factor in your health and mobility needs as you age.

3. Take Inventory: Take inventory of your possessions, separating them into categories such as keep, donate, sell, and throw away. This will help you determine what you truly need and what can be let go of.

4. Start Small: Begin downsizing with small areas of your home, like a single closet or a small room. This will help you build momentum and avoid feeling overwhelmed.

5. Consider Storage Options: If you have items you still need to be ready to part with, consider renting a storage unit. This will allow you to keep your possessions safe and secure while you decide what to do with them.

6. Get Help: Don't hesitate to ask for help from friends, family, or professional organizers. A fresh perspective can help you decide what to keep and let go of.

7. Set Realistic Expectations: Downsizing is a process that takes time. Set realistic expectations and try to do only a little at a time.

8. Keep What Makes You Happy: Don't feel you must keep everything. Keep meaningful or meaningful items that bring you joy, even if they don't have a practical use.

Overall, downsizing is a fantastic way to simplify your life and reduce stress in retirement. By starting early, considering your future needs, taking inventory, starting small, considering storage options, getting help, setting realistic expectations, and keeping what makes you happy, you can make the downsizing process a positive experience.

Subchapter 19.2: Decluttering

As people retire, they often consider downsizing and decluttering their homes to make their lives simpler, easier, and less stressful. Here are some tips on how to downsize and declutter:

1. Start early: Start decluttering early to avoid getting overwhelmed. Begin with small areas, such as a single closet or dresser, and gradually move on to larger sizes.

2. Plan: Create a plan of action for decluttering. Decide on the areas of the house to be decluttered and set a timeline for each room. Create categories such as "keep," "donate," "discard," or "sell."

3. Be selective: Be selective while deciding what to keep. Keep only those items with sentimental or functional value. Discard items that are broken or have not been used in a year or more. Consider donating or selling items in good condition but no longer needed.

4. Divide items into categories: Divide the things into several categories, including clothes, books, accessories, equipment, gadgets, and paperwork. Label the types, pack the items, and keep them organized.

5. Consider space and organization: Consider the available space while decluttering. Prioritize items and keep those that are necessary and often used. Organize the remaining items systematically and neatly in the open space. Consider buying or building storage systems to keep the area tidy.

6. Take advantage of technology: Consider taking advantage of digital technology. Scan important documents, records, and photographs and store them electronically. This will reduce clutter and preserve memories for future generations.

7. Involve loved ones or professional organizers: Involve family members, friends, or professional organizers to help declutter. A neutral and fresh perspective can help you decide which items to keep or discard.

8. Make it a positive experience: Make decluttering a positive experience by listening to music, taking breaks for relaxation, or rewarding yourself at the end of each task. This will make the process less overwhelming and more enjoyable.

Downsizing and decluttering require careful planning, diligence, and a systematic approach. Start early, plan, be selective, divide items into categories, consider space and organization, take advantage of technology, involve loved ones or professional organizers, and make it a positive experience to make the process easier. A life with fewer possessions can be a lighter, more fulfilling experience in one's golden years.

Here are some websites, books, and valuable resources for downsizing and decluttering:

Websites:

AARP (www.aarp.org) - AARP offers a variety of resources and articles on downsizing and decluttering for seniors. They supply practical tips, guides, and checklists to help you navigate downsizing.

National Association of Senior Move Managers (www.nasmm.org) - NASMM is dedicated to helping seniors and their families with downsizing and relocating. Their website offers resources, tips, and a directory of professional senior move managers who can provide expert assistance.

SeniorAdvisor.com (www.senioradvisor.com) - SeniorAdvisor.com is an online platform that provides information and reviews on senior living communities. They also have articles and resources on downsizing, decluttering, and organizing your home.

Books:

"The Gentle Art of Swedish Death Cleaning: How to Free Yourself and Your Family from a Lifetime of Clutter" by Margareta Magnusson - This book offers a unique perspective on decluttering, emphasizing the importance of organizing and letting go of possessions to simplify your life and prepare for the future.

"Downsizing the Family Home: What to Save, What to Let Go" by Marni Jameson - This book provides practical advice and emotional support for navigating the downsizing process, including tips on sorting through belongings, managing family dynamics, and making decisions about what to keep or let go.

"The Life-Changing Magic of Tidying Up: The Japanese Art of Decluttering and Organizing" by Marie Kondo - While not explicitly focused on downsizing for retirement, this book offers a popular method for decluttering and organizing your home, emphasizing the importance of keeping only items that spark joy.

These resources will provide guidance, strategies, and inspiration to downsize and declutter your home effectively. Remember to approach the process with patience and seek professional help if needed.

Chapter 20: Alternating Living Arrangements: Cohousing

Cohousing is an alternative living arrangement that has gained popularity among retirees. It's a concept that involves living in a small community of like-minded people who share common goals and responsibilities. Cohousing is an intentional community designed to foster community living and social interaction while allowing residents to maintain privacy and independence. Here are some benefits and disadvantages of cohousing in retirement:

Subchapter 20.1: Benefits of Cohousing in Retirement:

1. Social Interaction: Cohousing provides plenty of opportunities for social interaction, vital for preventing feelings of loneliness and isolation in retirement. Cohousing communities often have communal spaces like shared dining rooms, living rooms, and gardens that encourage people to meet and socialize.

2. Shared Expenses: Cohousing can be more affordable than living independently since residents split the costs of shared amenities like maintenance, repairs, utilities, and public areas. This can help retirees on a fixed income stretch their retirement savings further.

3. Shared Responsibility: Living in cohousing requires residents to take responsibility for the community's maintenance and upkeep. This shared responsibility can be fulfilling and collaborative; residents can help each other with tasks like cooking, cleaning, and gardening.

4. Safety: Cohousing communities often have a shared security system or gated entrance, which can provide residents a sense of security and safety. Neighbors look out for each other, and it's often a tight-knit community where people feel safe and supported.

5. Intergenerational Living: Cohousing communities often have diverse ages and backgrounds. This intergenerational living can have many benefits, including reducing age discrimination, promoting diversity, and encouraging opportunities to gain experience from each other.

Subchapter 20.2: Disadvantages of Cohousing in Retirement:

1. Limited Privacy: Cohousing often involves smaller living spaces and communal areas. This can impact privacy, especially for those who prefer solitude. Sharing common spaces in cohousing may also require residents to adjust their expectations of privacy.

2. Shared Decision-Making: Cohousing communities rely on a collaborative and democratic decision-making process. This can sometimes be challenging since all residents may have differing views on the same issues, and compromises may need to be made. Consensus building can take time and effort.

3. Limited Autonomy: Cohousing means sharing spaces and amenities with other residents. This shared living arrangement means there are rules and regulations everyone must follow. Residents must be willing to accept limitations to their independence and autonomy in cohousing.

4. Limited Flexibility: Cohousing residents must agree to work together for shared spaces, maintenance, and decision-making. This means that individual preferences may need to be put aside for the greater good of the community. Co-cohousing can be an excellent possibility for retirees seeking a collaborative, intergenerational living environment with mutual support and shared responsibilities. While there are some disadvantages, the benefits can outweigh them and offer a unique and fulfilling way of life.

Here are some websites, books, and valuable resources for exploring cohousing in retirement:

Websites:

- Cohousing.org (www.cohousing.org) - Cohousing.org is a comprehensive resource for learning about cohousing communities. They provide information on the benefits of cohousing, steps to create a community, and a directory of existing communities.
- Senior Cohousing Handbook (www.seniorcohousinghandbook.com) - This website is dedicated to senior cohousing and offers resources, articles, and a directory of senior cohousing communities. It provides information on senior cohousing's benefits, challenges, and considerations.
- Next Avenue (www.nextavenue.org) - Next Avenue is an online resource focused on topics related to aging and retirement. They have articles and resources on alternative living arrangements, including cohousing, with insights and advice for seniors.

Books:

- "Creating Cohousing: Building Sustainable Communities" by Kathryn McCamant and Charles Durrett - This book provides a comprehensive guide to cohousing, including the design, development, and management of cohousing communities. It offers practical advice and real-life examples to inspire and inform those interested in cohousing.
- "The Senior Cohousing Handbook: A Community Approach to Independent Living" by Charles Durrett - This book focuses explicitly on cohousing for seniors and guides creating and living in a senior cohousing community. It

covers topics such as community dynamics, finance, and legal considerations.

- "Senior Cohousing: A Community Approach to Independent Living" by John Davis - This book explores senior cohousing and shares stories and experiences from various senior cohousing communities. It offers insights into the benefits and challenges of living in a cohousing community as a senior.

These resources will provide valuable information and guidance on exploring cohousing as an alternative living arrangement in retirement. Remember to research and visit different communities, engage in discussions, and assess whether cohousing aligns with your lifestyle preferences and goals.

Chapter 21: Identity Protection; Protecting From Predators

Identity theft is a serious crime that can have devastating consequences for individuals. It involves the unauthorized acquisition and use of someone else's personal information for fraud. Understanding the several types of identity theft is crucial in protecting yourself:

Subchapter 21.1 Types of Identity Theft

a) Financial Identity Theft: This identity theft involves criminals accessing an individual's financial accounts, credit cards, or other financial information to make unauthorized transactions or purchases. They may use stolen credit card details to make fraudulent online purchases or withdraw funds from bank accounts.

b) Medical Identity Theft: Medical identity theft occurs when someone steals another person's personal information to receive medical care, submit false insurance claims, or obtain prescription drugs. This theft can have severe implications for the victim, such as incorrect medical records and compromised healthcare services.

c) Social Security Identity Theft: In this type of theft, criminals use someone else's Social Security number to gain employment, apply for government benefits, or commit tax fraud. Victims may only become aware of the theft when they receive notifications about unpaid taxes or discrepancies in their Social Security records.

d) Child Identity Theft: Children's identities are often targeted because they have clean credit histories. Criminals may use their personal information, such as Social Security numbers, to open fraudulent accounts, obtain credit, or apply for government benefits. Since children rarely monitor their credit, this theft can go undetected for years.

Subchapter 21.2: Preventing Identity Theft

Protecting your personal information is crucial in preventing identity theft. By implementing the following practices, you can significantly reduce the risk of becoming a victim:

<u>Safeguard Personal Information</u>

One of the first steps in preventing identity theft is safeguarding your personal information. This includes:

a) Secure Document Storage: Keep sensitive documents such as Social Security cards, passports, and financial statements in a secure place, preferably in a locked drawer or safe. Avoid carrying unnecessary identification cards in your wallet or purse.

b) Shred Unwanted Documents: Before disposing of any documents containing personal information, such as credit card statements, bank statements, or medical records, shred them. This prevents dumpster divers or unauthorized individuals from gaining access to your information.

c) Be Wary of Phone Scams: Be cautious when receiving unsolicited phone calls requesting personal information. Legitimate organizations typically do not ask for sensitive information over the phone. If in doubt, hang up and call the organization directly using a trusted contact number.

d) Secure Online Accounts: Use strong, unique passwords for all your online accounts, including email, banking, and social media. Avoid using easily guessable passwords and enable two-factor authentication whenever possible. Additionally, be cautious when accessing personal information online using public Wi-Fi networks, as they may not be secure.

Subchapter 21.3: Monitor Financial Accounts

Regularly monitoring your financial accounts is essential for detecting suspicious activity early on. Here's what you can do:

a) Review Bank Statements: Carefully review your monthly bank and credit card statements. Look for any unauthorized charges, foreign transactions, or suspicious activity. If you notice anything unusual, report it to your financial institution immediately.

b) Check Credit Reports: Request a free credit report from each central credit bureau (Equifax, Experian, and TransUnion) annually or stagger them throughout the year. Review these reports for any foreign accounts, credit inquiries, or discrepancies. Monitoring your credit reports allows you to detect any signs of identity theft or fraudulent activity.

c) Consider Credit Monitoring Services: Consider enrolling in a credit monitoring service that provides real-time alerts for any changes or suspicious activities related to your credit. These services can notify you if someone tries to open a new account or amend your charges.

Subchapter 21.4: Be Cautious Online and Offline

In today's digital age, it's essential to be cautious both online and offline to protect your identity:

a) Be Skeptical of Emails and Links: Exercise caution when clicking links or downloading attachments from unfamiliar or suspicious emails. These may be phishing attempts aimed at tricking you into providing personal information. Verify the legitimacy of the email sender before taking any action.

b) Use Secure Websites: Ensure the website is secure when entering personal information online. Look for the padlock symbol in the browser's address bar and use websites with "https" in the URL, indicating a secure connection.

c) Limit Information Sharing: Be selective when sharing personal information, especially on social media platforms. Avoid posting sensitive details such as your full address, birth date, or financial information, as identity thieves can use this information.

d) Be Wary of Impersonators: Be cautious of individuals posing as representatives from legitimate organizations, such as banks or government agencies, requesting personal information. If in doubt, hang up or close the door and contact the organization using the official contact information.

Subchapter 21.5: Responding to Identity Theft

If you become a victim of identity theft, taking immediate action is crucial to minimize the damage. Here are the steps you should take:

<u>Contact the Relevant Parties</u>

a) Contact Financial Institutions: If you notice any unauthorized transactions or suspect that your financial accounts have been compromised, immediately contact your bank, credit card companies, and other financial institutions. They can freeze or close compromised accounts and issue new ones.

b) File a Police Report: Report the identity theft to your local law enforcement agency and provide them with all relevant documentation and evidence. This report can help establish a paper trail of the theft and assist in resolving any legal or financial implications.

c) Contact Credit Bureaus: Place a fraud alert on your credit reports by contacting one of the major credit bureaus. This alert will notify potential creditors to verify your identity before granting credit. Consider placing a credit freeze on your reports, restricting access to your credit information, and preventing new accounts from being opened without your consent.

d) Report to the Federal Trade Commission (FTC): File a complaint with the FTC at identitytheft.gov, which provides resources and assistance in recovering from identity theft. The FTC can also help you create an Identity Theft Report, crucial for resolving certain fraudulent accounts and obtaining legal protection.

Subchapter 21.6: Keep Detailed Records

Maintain a comprehensive record of your steps to resolve identity theft. This includes dates, times, names of individuals spoken to, and any reference numbers or case files provided. Keeping detailed records ensures you understand the actions taken and can provide evidence.

Continuously monitor your financial accounts and credit reports after resolving identity theft. Stay vigilant for any signs of recurring fraudulent activity. Regularly reviewing your statements and credit reports lets you catch any potential red flags early on and take immediate action if necessary.

<u>Here are some websites and resources where you can find more information about identity theft prevention, response, and resources:</u>

- Federal Trade Commission (FTC) Identity Theft Website: The FTC provides comprehensive resources on identity theft, including information on prevention, reporting, and recovery. Visit their website at www.identitytheft.gov.
- Identity Theft Resource Center (ITRC): The ITRC is a nonprofit organization that offers free assistance to identity theft victims and provides resources for prevention. Their website, www.idtheftcenter.org, offers valuable information, educational materials, and support.
- Consumer Financial Protection Bureau (CFPB): The CFPB has resources on identity theft prevention and steps to take if you're a victim. Visit their website at www.consumerfinance.gov for helpful guides and information.
- Experian Identity Theft Resources: Experian, one of the major credit bureaus, has a dedicated section on its website that provides articles, tips, and tools to help individuals protect themselves against identity theft. Explore their resources at www.experian.com/identity-theft.

- Equifax Identity Theft Protection: Equifax offers identity theft protection services and resources. Their website, www.equifax.com/personal/identity-theft-protection, provides information on prevention and steps to take if you suspect identity theft.
- TransUnion Identity Theft Support Center: TransUnion's website, www.transunion.com/idtheft, offers guidance on identity theft prevention, detection, and recovery. They also provide access to credit monitoring services and tools to help protect your identity.
- StaySafeOnline.org: This website, managed by the National Cyber Security Alliance, provides resources on online safety and identity theft prevention. Explore their identity theft section at www.staysafeonline.org/identity-theft.

Remember to exercise caution when accessing websites and providing personal information online. Stick to reputable sources and always ensure the websites you visit are secure.

Conclusion

Identity theft is a pervasive and damaging crime that can have long-lasting consequences for individuals. Individuals can significantly reduce their risk and protect themselves from predators by understanding the types of identity theft, implementing preventive measures, and knowing how to respond if victimized. Stay initiative-taking in safeguarding your personal information, monitor your accounts regularly, and take immediate action if you suspect any fraudulent activity. Remember, prevention and quick response are vital in mitigating the impact of identity theft.

Chapter 22: Financial Scams; How To Protect (Seniors)

Financial fraud targeting seniors has become increasingly prevalent in recent years. Scammers often view seniors as vulnerable targets due to their retirement savings, trustworthiness, and potentially diminished cognitive abilities. Seniors and their families must be aware of common financial scams and take proactive steps to protect themselves. This comprehensive guide will delve into various financial frauds and provide practical strategies for safeguarding seniors' economic well-being.

Subchapter 22.1: Understanding the Types of Financial Scams

a. Impersonation Scams: Fraudsters pretend to be government officials, bank representatives, or family members to gain trust and manipulate seniors into revealing personal information or sending money.

b. Sweepstakes/Lottery Scams: Seniors are enticed with promises of winning a substantial prize but must pay upfront fees or share personal information to claim the prize.

c. Investment Scams: Scammers offer fraudulent investment opportunities promising high returns with little to no risk, luring seniors into making substantial investments that ultimately result in financial losses.

d. Medicare/Healthcare Scams: Seniors receive calls or emails pretending to be from Medicare, requesting personal information or payment for services or coverage.

e. Romance Scams: Scammers exploit seniors' emotions by establishing fake romantic relationships online and requesting money for assorted reasons, such as medical emergencies or travel expenses.

f. The utility scam: A scammer pretends to be from your electric or telephone company, tells you your bill is overdue, and threatens to cut off your service if you don't pay immediately.

g. The charity scam: A scammer calls or approaches you soliciting donations for a fake charity or organization.

h. The grandparent scam: A scammer calls you and pretends to be your grandchild, sharing a "personal" story with you before asking you for money.

Subchapter 22.2: Understanding the Types of Financial Scams

<u>Warning Signs of Financial Scams:</u>

a. Unsolicited calls or emails: Avoid any unexpected communication requesting personal information, money, or investments.

b. Urgency or pressure: Scammers often create a sense of urgency, pressuring seniors to act quickly without providing time for careful consideration.

c. Requests for payment via unconventional methods: Scammers may ask for a price through wire transfers, gift cards, or cryptocurrency, as these methods are difficult to trace.

d. Poor grammar or spelling: Many scams originate overseas, so that poor language skills may indicate fraudulent activity.

e. Promises of unusually high returns: If an investment opportunity seems too good to be true, it probably is.

f. Requests for upfront payments: A common tactic among scammers is to ask for upfront costs or fees for services not provided. For example, you might be asked to pay an insurance fee before a loan can be approved or a processing fee for a promise of huge profits. Unfortunately, once you make the payment, the scammer disappears.

g. Suspicious links or attachments: Scammers often use infected links or attachments to install malware on your computer, steal your identity, or get access to your sensitive information. Be wary when an email contains suspicious links or attachments, and don't click on them unless you're sure it's a legitimate source.

Subchapter 22.3: Understanding the Types of Financial Scams

Strategies to Protect Seniors from Financial Scams:

a. Educate seniors: Provide comprehensive information about common financial scams, warning signs, and prevention strategies. Encourage open communication and ensure seniors feel comfortable discussing suspicious activities or requests.

b. Strengthen privacy measures: Advise seniors to safeguard personal information, such as Social Security numbers, bank account details, and Medicare numbers. Please encourage them to shred sensitive documents and avoid sharing personal information online.

c. Utilize caller ID and call-blocking: Advise seniors to use caller ID to screen incoming calls and encourage them to block suspicious or unknown numbers. Register their phone numbers with the National Do Not Call Registry to reduce telemarketing calls.

d. Stay updated on scams: Seniors should regularly access reputable sources of information, such as the Federal Trade Commission (FTC) and local law enforcement websites, to stay informed about the latest scams.

e. Create a support network: Encourage seniors to involve trusted family members, friends, or financial advisors in their financial decisions. This network can help validate suspicious requests and provide guidance.

Subchapter 22.4: Reporting Scams:

a. Federal Trade Commission (FTC): In the United States, seniors can report scams to the FTC online at www.ftc.gov/complaint or by phone at 1-877-FTC-HELP.

b. Local law enforcement: Seniors should report scams to their local police department or state attorney general's office.

c. Better Business Bureau (BBB): Seniors can file complaints and report scams to the BBB, which tracks fraudulent activities and helps protect consumers.

Here are some websites and resources where you can find more information about financial scams and how to protect seniors:

- Federal Trade Commission (FTC): The FTC provides extensive information on several types of scams targeting seniors and offers resources for prevention and reporting. Visit their website at www.ftc.gov and search for "Protecting Older Adults" or "Avoiding Scams" to access their dedicated help.
- Consumer Financial Protection Bureau (CFPB): The CFPB has a section on its website dedicated to protecting older adults from financial exploitation. It offers guides, resources, and tips on recognizing and preventing scams. Visit www.consumerfinance.gov and search for "Protecting Older Adults" to access the relevant information.
- National Council on Aging (NCOA): The NCOA provides resources and educational materials on financial scams targeting seniors. Their website, www.ncoa.org, offers information on common scams, prevention strategies, and assistance programs for seniors.
- AARP Fraud Watch Network: AARP's Fraud Watch Network focuses on raising awareness about scams and provides resources to help seniors avoid falling victim. Visit

www.aarp.org/fraudwatchnetwork to access articles, scam alerts, and prevention tips.

- Better Business Bureau (BBB) Scam Tracker: The BBB Scam Tracker allows you to report and search for scams targeting seniors in your area. It provides valuable information on recent scams, enabling users to stay updated on emerging threats. Visit www.bbb.org/scamtracker to explore the tool.
- Stop Fraud Colorado: This website, www.stopfraudcolorado.gov, offers resources specific to Colorado but contains valuable information applicable to anyone looking to protect themselves or their loved ones from financial scams. It includes tips, news updates, and reporting options.
- Local Law Enforcement Agencies: Check your local law enforcement agency's website or contact them directly to inquire about resources and programs available to protect seniors from financial scams. They may offer educational materials, workshops, or community outreach initiatives.

Remember, staying informed and educated is crucial in protecting yourself and your loved ones from financial scams. Be cautious, verify information independently, and report any suspicious activities to the appropriate authorities.

Conclusion:

Financial scams targeting seniors significantly threaten their financial security and well-being. Seniors and their loved ones must proactively protect themselves against these scams. By understanding the several types of scams, recognizing warning signs, and implementing protective strategies, seniors can minimize their vulnerability and safeguard their financial assets.

Education and awareness play a vital role in preventing financial scams. Seniors should be provided comprehensive information about various scams, including how scammers operate and their tactics. Family members, caregivers, and community organizations can organize workshops or informational sessions to educate seniors about these risks. Emphasize the importance of skepticism and encourage seniors to question unsolicited requests for personal information or money.

Privacy protection is another critical aspect of safeguarding against financial scams. Seniors should be advised to keep their personal information private and to exercise caution when sharing it, even with seemingly trustworthy individuals or organizations. Remind them to shred documents containing sensitive information before discarding them and to be cautious about sharing personal details online, especially on social media platforms.

Technological tools can also be utilized to protect seniors from scams. Advise seniors to use caller ID to screen incoming calls and recommend installing call-blocking applications to prevent unwanted or suspicious calls. Additionally, guide them on registering their phone numbers with the National Do Not Call Registry, which can reduce the number of telemarketing calls they receive.

Staying informed about the latest scams is crucial for seniors' protection. Please encourage them to regularly visit reputable websites, such as the Federal Trade Commission (FTC) or local law enforcement websites, which provide up-to-date information about scams and offer resources for reporting fraudulent activities. These sources often publish alerts about new scams and provide tips on how to avoid falling victim to them.

Creating a support network is invaluable for seniors in preventing financial scams. Please encourage them to involve trusted family members, friends, or financial advisors in their financial decisions. This network can serve as an additional layer of protection by validating suspicious requests and providing guidance when seniors need clarification on the legitimacy of specific offers or opportunities.

If a senior falls victim to a financial scam, it is crucial to report the incident promptly. Seniors should be aware of the reporting options available to them. They can report scams to the Federal Trade Commission (FTC) online at www.ftc.gov/complaint or by phone at 1-877-FTC-HELP. Additionally, they should contact their local police department or state attorney general's office to file a report. Reporting scams to organizations like the Better Business Bureau (BBB) can also help track fraudulent activities and protect other consumers.

In conclusion, protecting seniors from financial scams requires a multi-faceted approach that includes education, privacy protection, technological tools, staying informed, and creating a support network. By implementing these strategies and remaining vigilant, seniors can significantly reduce their risk of falling victim to scams and safeguard their financial well-being. Seniors and their loved ones must work together to combat financial scams and promote a safe and secure environment for seniors' financial affairs.

Chapter 23: Senior Discounts; How To Find And Maximize.

This chapter delves into senior discounts and provides valuable information on how to find and maximize these discounts. As seniors enter retirement, managing expenses becomes a crucial aspect of financial planning. Senior discounts offer a way to save money and make retirement more affordable. This chapter explores various strategies, tips, and resources to help seniors take advantage of discounts available in different areas of life.

Subchapter 23.1: Understanding Senior Discounts

In this section, we provide an overview of what senior discounts are and how they work. We explain that senior discounts are unique offers and reduced prices available to individuals of a certain age (typically fifty-five or older). Businesses, organizations, and service providers can offer these discounts to attract and reward senior customers. It's important to note that the availability and extent of discounts may vary depending on the location, business, and specific terms and conditions.

Subchapter 23.2: Types of Senior Discounts

Here, we delve into the several types of senior discounts that seniors can use. We cover a wide range of areas, including:

R, retail and Grocery Stores: Many retail stores and supermarkets offer senior discounts on specific days of the week or month. Some provide a flat percentage discount, while others may have special promotions or loyalty programs for seniors.

Restaurants and Dining: Seniors can enjoy discounts at various restaurants, coffee shops, and fast-food chains. These discounts may apply to specific meals, menu items, or dining times.

Travel and Transportation: Seniors often receive discounted rates on flights, hotels, rental cars, and public transportation. We explore travel-related discounts, such as senior fares and special packages for seniors.

Entertainment and Leisure: This section offers discounts on movie tickets, museums, theaters, concerts, theme parks, and other recreational activities. We provide examples of popular venues that offer senior discounts and highlight any specific requirements or limitations.

Health and Wellness: Seniors can benefit from discounts on gym memberships, fitness classes, spa services, and even medical supplies. We discuss how to find these discounts and the potential health benefits of staying active in retirement.

Insurance and Financial Services: Some insurance companies and financial institutions offer discounts or special packages tailored for seniors. We explore options and highlight the importance of reviewing insurance policies and financial plans regularly.

Subchapter 23.3: Finding Senior Discounts

In this section, we provide practical advice on how to find senior discounts. We suggest the following strategies:

Research Online: Many websites and platforms compile lists of senior discounts in various categories. Popular websites like SeniorDiscounts.com, TheSeniorList.com, and BenefitsCheckUp.org provide comprehensive databases and search tools.

Join Senior Organizations: Becoming a member of senior organizations like AARP (American Association of Retired Persons) or AAA (American Automobile Association) can offer access to exclusive discounts and benefits.

Inquire Locally: Local businesses, community centers, and senior centers often offer discounts, but they may need to be more widely advertised. We encourage seniors to inquire about discounts when shopping locally or using local services.

Sign up for Newsletters and Mailing Lists: Many businesses and organizations send newsletters or emails with information about discounts and promotions. We advise signing up for these mailing lists to stay informed about the latest deals.

Ask for Senior Discounts: Sometimes, senior discounts are not explicitly advertised. We encourage seniors to ask businesses and service providers if they offer any discounts for seniors. It's surprising how many places offer discounts but may need to promote them more actively.

Subchapter 23.4: Maximizing Senior Discounts

In this section, we provide tips and tricks to help seniors maximize their savings with senior discounts:

Combine Discounts: Some businesses allow the stacking of discounts, so it's worth inquiring whether multiple values can be applied to a purchase. For example, using a senior discount in h a store coupon can lead to even more significant savings.

Timing Matters: Knowing specific days or times when discounts are offered can help seniors plan their purchases strategically. For instance, some restaurants may have early bird specials or discounted lunch menus.

Loyalty Programs: Joining loyalty programs offered by retailers, restaurants, or service providers can lead to additional discounts and perks. These programs often provide exclusive offers and accumulate points or rewards for future savings.

Stay Informed: Senior discounts can change, and new values may become available. We advise staying updated by regularly checking websites, signing up for newsletters, and following the social media accounts of businesses and organizations that offer senior discounts.

Subchapter 23.5: Pros and Cons of Senior Discounts

In this section, we explore the pros and cons of senior discounts to provide a balanced view:

Pros:

Cost Savings: Senior discounts help reduce expenses and make retirement more affordable.

Appreciation and Recognition: Discounts for seniors acknowledge their contributions and provide a sense of recognition and value.

Increased Access: Discounts make various products, services, and experiences more accessible to seniors.

Social Opportunities: Senior discounts can encourage seniors to engage in social activities and explore new interests.

Cons:

Limited Availability: Not all businesses or service providers offer senior discounts, and the extent of values can vary.

Age Restrictions: Senior discounts are generally available to individuals of a specific age, which may exclude younger retirees.

Potential Stigma: Some seniors may feel hesitant or embarrassed to ask for discounts, considering it a reminder of their age.

Restrictions and Limitations: Discounts may have restrictions on usage, such as specific days, times, or qualifying criteria.

Conclusion:

The importance of senior discounts in retirement planning provides practical advice on finding and maximizing these discounts. By taking advantage of senior discounts, retirees can stretch their budgets, enjoy various products and services at reduced costs, and enhance their overall quality of life. Seniors must explore event avenues for discounts, stay informed about new opportunities, and maximize the savings available. Remember little bit counts in creating a fulfilling and financially secure retirement.

<u>Here are some famous clubs, membership organizations, and websites that offer resources and information on senior discounts:</u>

- AARP (American Association of Retired Persons): AARP is one of the largest and most well-known organizations for seniors, offering various benefits, discounts, and resources. They provide information on multiple aspects of retirement, including senior discounts, health care, travel, and more. Their website is a valuable resource for finding bargains and exploring other opportunities: https://www.aarp.org/

- AAA (American Automobile Association): While primarily known for its roadside assistance services, AAA also offers discounts on travel, dining, entertainment, and more. Their membership provides access to a range of benefits for seniors. Visit their website for more information: https://www.aaa.com/

- SeniorDiscounts.com: This website compiles an extensive database of senior discounts across various categories. They provide information on discounts available at restaurants, retailers, travel destinations, and other establishments. Their website allows you to search for deals by location or category: https://seniordiscounts.com

- SeniorAdvisor.com: SeniorAdvisor.com is a platform that offers reviews and information on senior living communities, home care services, and senior-friendly businesses. They also provide a section dedicated explicitly to senior discounts and promotions: https://www.senioradvisor.com/senior-discounts

- The Senior List: The Senior List is a website that provides seniors with resources, information, and advice. They offer a section dedicated to senior discounts, highlighting various discounts available for multiple categories and locations: https://www.theseniorlist.com/

- Benefits Checkup: Benefits Checkup, provided by the National Council on Aging, is a comprehensive online tool that helps seniors find benefit programs they may be eligible for, including discounts and assistance programs. It allows you to search for available benefits based on your location and personal circumstances: https://www.benefitscheckup.org/

Remember also to check specific businesses and establishments, as many may offer their senior discount programs. Additionally, local senior centers or community organizations in your area may have information on exclusive discounts available to seniors. Please note that while these resources are accurate and reputable as of my knowledge cutoff in September 2021, verifying the information, checking for updates on the respective websites, or contacting the organizations directly for the most current information is always an innovative idea.

Conclusion:

Senior discounts are a valuable resource for retirees, allowing them to save money while enjoying various products, services, and experiences. You can maximize your savings and retirement budget by identifying discount programs, utilizing membership organizations, inquiring about discounts, utilizing online resources, and combining offers. Remember always to carry identification, be proactive in seeking discounts, and enjoy the perks and benefits of being a senior. With these strategies and insights, you can confidently navigate the world of senior discounts and enhance your retirement lifestyle.

Chapter 24: Estate Planning and Legal Considerations

Estate planning involves making important decisions about your assets, beneficiaries, and legal matters to ensure your wishes are conducted and your loved ones are cared for. This chapter explores the importance of estate planning, the role of wills, trusts, and power of attorney, and considerations related to beneficiary designations and estate taxes.

Subchapter 24.1: Importance of Estate Planning

Estate planning is essential regardless of the size of your estate. It allows you to control how your assets are distributed and ensure your loved ones are cared for according to your wishes. Here's why estate planning is essential:

Asset Distribution: Estate planning lets you specify who will inherit your assets and in what proportion. It provides a clear plan for distributing your property, including financial support, real estate, personal belongings, and digital assets. Without a proper estate plan, state laws will determine how your assets are distributed, which may not align with your intentions.

Guardianship for Dependents: If you have minor children or dependents with special needs, estate planning allows you to designate a guardian to care for them in case of incapacitation or death. This ensures that their well-being is protected and that someone they trust is responsible for their upbringing and support.

Minimizing Conflict and Expenses: A well-crafted estate plan can help minimize conflicts and reduce legal expenses for your loved ones. It provides clear instructions, minimizes the potential for disputes among family members, and avoids the need for costly court proceedings.

Subchapter 24.2: Wills, Trusts, and Power of Attorney

Wills, trusts, and power of attorney are essential legal instruments in estate planning. Here's an overview of their roles and importance:

Wills: A legal document will outline your wishes regarding asset distribution, guardianship for dependents, and other vital instructions. It allows you to name an executor responsible for your desires and settling your estate. A will provides clarity and legal validity to your intentions and is an essential component of an estate plan.

Trusts: A trust is a legal arrangement that allows you to transfer assets to a trustee who manages and distributes them according to your instructions. Trusts can provide benefits such as avoiding probate, minimizing estate taxes, and providing ongoing financial support to beneficiaries. Trusts can be revocable or irrevocable, depending on your needs and objectives.

Power of Attorney: Power of attorney is a legal document that designates someone (an agent or attorney-in-fact) to make financial or healthcare decisions on your behalf in the event of your incapacitation. It is crucial to have power of attorney to ensure that your affairs are managed by a trusted individual who can act in your best interests when you cannot.

Subchapter 24.3: Beneficiary Designations and Estate Tax Considerations

In addition to wills, trusts, and power of attorney, estate planning involves considerations related to beneficiary designations and estate taxes. Here's what you need to know:

Beneficiary Designations: Many assets, such as life insurance policies, retirement accounts, and bank accounts, allow you to designate beneficiaries who will receive the assets upon death. Reviewing and updating these beneficiary designations periodically ensures they align with your current wishes. Failure to set or update beneficiaries can result in unintended consequences or delays in asset distribution.

Estate Tax Considerations: Estate taxes are taxes imposed on the value of an estate upon the owner's death. While not everyone is subject to estate taxes, it's essential to consider the potential impact on your estate and take necessary steps to minimize the tax burden. Here are some key points to consider:

Estate Tax Exemption: Familiarize yourself with the tax exemption limit the government sets. This is the threshold above which estate taxes may be imposed. As of my knowledge cutoff in September 2021, the exemption limit was high, but staying updated with the latest regulations is always prudent.

Tax Planning Strategies: Work with a qualified estate planning attorney or tax professional to explore tax planning strategies that can help minimize estate taxes. These strategies may include gifting assets during your lifetime, establishing irrevocable trusts, or utilizing charitable giving strategies.

State-Specific Considerations: Remember that some states have estate tax laws with different exemption limits and tax rates. Research the specific regulations in your state to understand any additional considerations you may need to address.

Seek Professional Guidance: Estate planning and tax laws can be complex, so consulting with professionals specializing in estate planning and taxation is advisable. They can provide guidance tailored to your circumstances and ensure your estate plan complies with the law.

Remember that estate planning is a dynamic process, and it's essential to review and update your estate plan periodically or whenever significant life events occur, such as marriage, divorce, the birth of children or grandchildren, or changes in financial circumstances. By addressing wills, trusts, power of attorney, beneficiary designations, and estate tax considerations, you can create a comprehensive estate plan that reflects your wishes and helps protect your assets and loved ones.

Here are some valuable resources, including websites and books, for Estate Planning and Legal Considerations:

Websites:

- American Bar Association - Section of Real Property, Trust, and Estate Law: The ABA's website provides a wealth of information on estate planning, including articles, guides, and resources for finding an estate planning attorney. Visit their website at americanbar.org/
- National Association of Estate Planners & Councils: This organization offers resources for finding estate planning professionals, educational materials, and articles on estate planning topics. Their website is naepc.org.

Books:

- "Estate Planning Basics" by Denis Clifford: This book provides a comprehensive overview of estate planning, covering topics such as wills, trusts, probate, and more. It offers practical guidance for creating an effective estate plan.
- "Plan Your Estate" by Denis Clifford: Another excellent resource by Denis Clifford, this book delves deeper into estate planning strategies, including legal considerations, minimizing taxes, and protecting assets.
- "Estate Planning for Dummies" by N. Brian Caverly and Jordan S. Simon: This beginner-friendly guide explains estate planning concepts, helping readers navigate the complexities of wills, trusts, and other legal documents.

Valuable Resources:

- The Estate Planning Source: This online resource offers articles, FAQs, and estate planning tools to help individuals understand and plan their estates effectively. Visit their website at estateplanningsource.com.
- Elder Law Answers: This website specializes in legal issues affecting seniors and offers information on estate planning, long-term care, Medicaid, and more. Visit their website at elderlawanswers.com.
- Your State Bar Association: Check your local State Bar Association's website, as many provide resources and information on estate planning specific to your state. They may also have directories to help you find qualified estate planning attorneys.

Remember, estate planning is a complex area, and it's always advisable to consult an experienced estate planning attorney to ensure your plans align with your specific circumstances and goals. These resources can provide valuable insights and information, but personalized legal advice is crucial for estate planning.

Chapter 25: Family Relationships; Solving Family Conflicts in Retirement

Retirement is a significant life transition that can bring joy and challenges to family dynamics. As individuals retire or retire, it is vital to maintain strong family relationships and resolve conflicts effectively. This chapter will explore real-world scenarios and provide actionable advice from someone in retirement or thinking about retirement shortly.

Subchapter 25.1: Communication and Understanding

Scenario 1: Parent-Child Financial Disagreements

John, a retiree, and his adult children often find themselves in conflicts regarding financial matters, such as inheritance and support.

Actionable Advice:

<u>Open and Transparent Communication</u>: Encourage John and his children to converse honestly about financial expectations, retirement plans, and long-term care. Clear communication can help prevent misunderstandings and resolve conflicts before they escalate.

<u>Seek Professional Advice</u>: Suggest consulting a financial planner or estate attorney to guide inheritance planning, fiscal management, and creating a comprehensive plan that aligns with everyone's needs and goals.

<u>Mediation:</u> If conflicts persist, recommend involving a mediator who can facilitate conversations and help find mutually agreeable solutions that balance John's financial security and his children's concerns.

<u>Compromise and Fairness:</u> Encourage John and his children to approach financial matters fairly and compromise. Considering

everyone's needs and aspirations can lead to more harmonious outcomes.

Scenario 2: Balancing Autonomy and Support

Elizabeth, a retiree, and her adult children often struggle to balance Elizabeth's desire for independence and her children's willingness to support and care for her.

Actionable Advice:

Respect Autonomy: Emphasize the importance of respecting Elizabeth's autonomy and allowing her to make decisions regarding her retirement, living arrangements, and daily activities. Encourage open dialogue to understand her desires and concerns.

Emotional Support: Remind Elizabeth's children to offer emotional support, reassurance, and understanding. Assure Elizabeth that her children's concern stems from love and care, not a desire to control.

Collaborative Decision-Making: Encourage Elizabeth and her children to collaborate on decisions that affect her well-being. This can include involving her children in discussions about health care planning, long-term care options, or downsizing.

Regular Check-Ins: Recommend regular family meetings or check-ins to maintain open lines of communication and address any emerging concerns. This fosters a sense of connection and ensures everyone's needs are considered.

Subchapter 25.2: Managing Conflict and Building Resilience

Scenario 1: Generation Gap and Communication Styles

Richard, a retiree, often experiences conflicts with his grandchildren due to a generation gap and differences in communication styles and interests.

Actionable Advice:

<u>Bridge the Generation Gap:</u> Encourage Richard to actively engage with his grandchildren, showing interest in their hobbies, technology, and pop culture. This can help build common ground and understanding.

<u>Flexible Communication:</u> Remind Richard to be flexible in his communication style, adapting to the preferences and modes of communication his grandchildren prefer, such as texting, video calls, or social media platforms.

<u>Mutual Learning:</u> Encourage Richard and his grandchildren to learn from each other. Richard can share his life experiences and wisdom, while the grandchildren can offer insights into the modern world and new perspectives.

<u>Respectful Boundaries:</u> Ensure Richard and his grandchildren respect each other's boundaries and personal space. This includes understanding each other's need for privacy and alone time.

Scenario 2: Health and Aging Concerns

Susan, a retiree, often experiences conflicts with her adult children regarding her health and aging-related decisions, such as medical treatment and assisted living options.

Actionable Advice:

<u>Early Planning:</u> Encourage Susan and her adult children to plan early for her future healthcare needs and aging-related decisions. This can involve discussing preferences for medical treatment, creating advance directives, and exploring diverse options for assisted living or long-term care.

<u>Family Meetings:</u> Suggest holding regular family meetings to discuss Susan's health concerns and care plans. This provides an opportunity for open communication, understanding each other's perspectives, and finding common ground.

<u>Professional Guidance:</u> Advise Susan and her adult children to seek guidance from healthcare professionals, geriatric care managers, or social workers specializing in aging-related issues. Their expertise can

offer insights, mediate discussions, and provide resources for making informed decisions.

<u>Empathy and Support:</u> Encourage Susan's adult children to approach conflicts with compassion, understanding the emotional challenges Susan may face as she ages. Providing emotional support and actively involving Susan in decision-making can help foster a sense of autonomy and reduce conflicts.

Conclusion:

Maintaining strong family relationships becomes even more crucial as individuals retire or retire. Conflicts can be resolved effectively by prioritizing open communication, empathy, and understanding, fostering harmonious family dynamics during this significant life phase.

Here are some valuable resources, including websites, books, and other materials, for "Family Relationships: Solving Family Conflicts in Retirement":

Websites:

ElderCare Online (eldercareonline.com): This website offers articles, forums, and resources specifically focused on addressing family conflicts in eldercare situations. It provides insights and strategies for managing conflicts and improving family relationships.

Psychology Today (psychologytoday.com): Psychology Today covers various topics related to psychology and relationships. You can find articles and resources specifically related to family conflicts, communication, and resolving issues within the family.

Family Caregiver Alliance (caregiver.org): This organization provides resources and support for family caregivers. They offer articles, fact sheets, and online support groups that address and guide resolving family conflicts.

Books:

"Difficult Conversations: How to Discuss What Matters Most" by Douglas Stone, Bruce Patton, and Sheila Heen: This book provides practical guidance on having challenging conversations and resolving conflicts. It offers strategies for effective communication and problem-solving within the family.

"Crucial Conversations: Tools for Talking When Stakes Are High" by Kerry Patterson, Joseph Grenny, Ron McMillan, and Al Switzler: This book offers insights and techniques for handling difficult conversations and resolving conflicts in various areas of life, including family relationships.

"When Aging Parents Can't Live Alone: A Practical Family Guide" by Ellen F. Rubenson: This book focuses on navigating family conflicts and making decisions about caregiving and living arrangements for aging parents. It provides practical advice and tools for resolving disputes and finding solutions that work for everyone involved.

Valuable Resources:

Mediation and Conflict Resolution Centers: Local mediation centers often provide services to help families resolve conflicts and improve communication. They offer trained mediators who can facilitate discussions and assist in finding mutually agreeable solutions.

Family Therapists or Counselors: Seeking the help of a qualified family therapist or counselor can be beneficial in navigating family conflicts. They can provide guidance, mediation, and tools to improve communication and address underlying issues.

Remember, family conflicts can be emotionally challenging, and seeking professional guidance or support from mediators, therapists, or counselors can often help resolve disputes, disputes, s then family relationships.

Chapter 26: Life Insurance; Alternative To Term in Retirement

Retirement is when individuals reassess their financial plans, including their insurance coverage. Life insurance plays a crucial role in providing financial security for loved ones in the event of the policyholder's death. In this chapter, we will explore real-world scenarios and provide actionable advice from the perspective of someone in retirement or considering retirement, focusing on alternatives to term life insurance in retirement.

Subchapter 26.1: Understanding Life Insurance Needs in Retirement

Scenario 1: Ensuring Spouse's Financial Security

John, a retiree, wants to ensure that his spouse, Susan, will have sufficient financial support during his death. However, he is still determining whether term life insurance is the most suitable option.

Actionable Advice:

Evaluate Current Financial Situation: Begin by assessing John and Susan's current financial situation, including their retirement savings, pension, and any other sources of income. This analysis will help determine if additional life insurance coverage is necessary.

Consider Permanent Life Insurance: In retirement, permanent life insurance, such as whole or universal life, may be more appropriate than term life insurance. Permanent policies cover the insured's entire lifetime and can build cash value over time, offering protection and potential financial benefits.

Consult with a Financial Advisor: Engage the services of a financial advisor specializing in retirement planning and life insurance. They can assess John and Susan's needs, considering their goals, current assets, and desired level of financial protection.

<u>Review Existing Policies:</u> If John already has a term life insurance policy, he should review its terms and consider converting it to a permanent policy or explore the option of purchasing a new one to meet their evolving needs.

Scenario 2: Legacy Planning and Estate Protection

Emily is a retiree who wishes to leave a financial legacy for her children and grandchildren while protecting her estate from potential tax liabilities.

Actionable Advice:

<u>Estate Planning and Tax Considerations:</u> Work with an estate planning attorney to create a comprehensive estate plan that aligns with Emily's goals. This includes considering tax-efficient strategies to minimize estate taxes and maximize the wealth transferred to beneficiaries.

<u>Permanent Life Insurance for Estate Protection:</u> Permanent life insurance can be an effective tool for estate protection. A policy with a death benefit equal to or greater than the estimated estate tax liability can provide liquidity to pay estate taxes, allowing Emily's heirs to inherit the estate without burden.

<u>Trusts and Life Insurance:</u> Explore using irrevocable life insurance trusts (ILITs) to own the insurance policy. This arrangement helps keep the policy proceeds outside the taxable estate and provides flexibility in distributing the death benefit to beneficiaries.

<u>Periodic Policy Review:</u> Regularly review the life insurance policy and estate plan to ensure they remain aligned with Emily's wishes and changing tax laws. Periodic reassessment will allow for adjustments as needed.

Subchapter 26.2: Maximizing Life Insurance Benefits in Retirement

Scenario 1: Supplementing Retirement Income

William, a retiree, is concerned about having enough income to support his desired lifestyle and cover potential long-term care expenses.

Actionable Advice:

<u>Consider Life Insurance with Living Benefits:</u> Explore purchasing a permanent life insurance policy that offers living benefits, such as accelerated death benefits or long-term care riders. These features allow William to access a portion of the death benefit to cover qualifying long-term care expenses or supplement retirement income in case of chronic illness.

<u>Evaluate Risk Tolerance:</u> Assess William's risk tolerance and capacity for investment. He may consider purchasing a variable universal life insurance policy that allows him to allocate premiums to investment accounts, potentially increasing the cash value and providing a source of supplemental income in retirement.

<u>Consult a Financial Planner:</u> Engage the services of a financial planner specializing in retirement income planning and life insurance. They can help analyze William's income needs, assess the viability of different life insurance options, and create a strategy to maximize his retirement income.

<u>Review Policy Performance:</u> Review the life insurance policy's performance regularly, considering any living benefits or investment components. This will ensure that the policy continues to meet William's income needs and adjust as necessary.

Scenario 2: Charitable Giving and Philanthropy

Elizabeth, a retiree, desires to leave a charitable legacy and support causes close to her heart through life insurance.

Actionable Advice:

<u>Research Charitable Life Insurance Options:</u> Explore charitable life insurance programs from reputable organizations and foundations. These programs allow Elizabeth to make a substantial gift to her chosen

charity while potentially providing her with tax benefits during her lifetime.

<u>Work with a Philanthropic Advisor:</u> Seek guidance from a philanthropic advisor specializing in charitable giving and life insurance planning. They can help Elizabeth identify suitable organizations, navigate tax implications, and structure the life insurance policy to align with her philanthropic goals.

<u>Ensure Policy Ownership and Beneficiary Designations:</u> Carefully consider the ownership and beneficiary designations of the life insurance policy. In some cases, it may be beneficial to transfer ownership to the charity or create a charitable remainder trust (CRT) that receives the policy proceeds.

<u>Ongoing Engagement and Review:</u> Maintain regular communication with the chosen charity and periodically review the life insurance policy to ensure it remains aligned with Elizabeth's philanthropic objectives.

Here are some websites and sources where you can find information about life insurance alternatives to term insurance in retirement:

Investopedia (www.investopedia.com): Investopedia is a comprehensive financial resource that provides articles, guides, and tools to help individuals understand and make informed decisions about various financial topics. They have a dedicated life insurance section covering several types of policies, including alternatives to term insurance.

The Balance (www.thebalance.com): The Balance is a personal finance website that offers a wide range of articles and resources on insurance and retirement planning. They have a section on life insurance, where you can find information about different policies suitable for retirees.

Policygenius (www.policygenius.com): Policygenius is an online insurance marketplace that allows individuals to compare and shop for several types of insurance, including life insurance. They provide educational resources, guides, and articles on life insurance options for retirees.

AARP (www.aarp.org): AARP is a nonprofit organization focused on advocating for the needs and interests of older adults. Their website offers a wealth of information on various retirement-related topics, including insurance. They have articles and resources that cover life insurance options for retirees.

Life Happens (www.lifehappens.org): Life Happens is a nonprofit organization dedicated to raising awareness about the importance of life insurance and other related financial planning topics. They offer educational resources, calculators, and articles on life insurance options for different life stages, including retirement.

Insurance company websites: Many insurance companies have informative websites that provide details about their life insurance products, including alternatives to term insurance. Companies like Prudential, MetLife, and New York Life often have resources tailored explicitly to retirees on their websites.

It's important to note that while these sources can provide valuable information, consulting with a financial advisor or insurance professional who can assess your needs and provide personalized guidance based on your circumstances is always recommended.

Conclusion:

As retirement approaches or is being considered, evaluating life insurance needs and exploring alternatives to term life insurance that align with retirement goals is essential. Retirees can ensure the financial security, protect their estates, supplement retirement income, and even leave a lasting charitable legacy by seeking professional advice, assessing individual circumstances, and tailoring life insurance strategies accordingly.

Chapter 27: Coping With the Death Of a Spouse Or Loved One in Retirement

Losing a spouse or loved one is a profoundly challenging experience that can significantly impact individuals in retirement. This chapter aims to provide detailed guidance and support for navigating the grieving process and finding ways to cope with loss during retirement. It will explore various aspects of grief, including emotional, practical, and financial considerations, and offer real-world scenarios, advice, tips, and tricks to help individuals through this challenging time.

Subchapter 27.1: Understanding Grief and its Impact.

Overview of the grieving process: Grief is a natural response to loss, and understanding the stages of grief can provide individuals with a framework for their journey. The steps, including shock, denial, anger, depression, and acceptance, are not linear and may vary from person to person. Individuals can better navigate their emotions and experiences by recognizing and acknowledging these stages.

Emotional impact: Losing a spouse or loved one can evoke intense emotions, such as sadness, loneliness, guilt, and anxiety. It is crucial to validate these emotions and permit oneself to grieve. Seeking support through therapy, support groups, or counseling services can provide a safe space to express and process these feelings.

Physical and mental well-being: Grief can affect physical and psychological health. Taking care of oneself becomes paramount during this time. Engaging in regular exercise, maintaining a balanced diet, and getting enough rest can contribute to overall well-being. Finding a healthy outlet for expressing emotions, such as journaling or engaging in creative activities, can support healing.

Social support: Building and maintaining a support network is crucial during loss. Connecting with family, friends, and community resources can provide emotional support and companionship. Joining support groups designed for individuals who have lost a spouse or loved one can offer a sense of understanding and solidarity.

Subchapter 27.2: Practical Considerations

Legal and financial matters: Various legal and financial considerations exist after losing a spouse or loved one. Updating legal documents, such as wills and beneficiary designations, is essential to reflect the new circumstances. Reviewing financial arrangements, such as insurance policies, investments, and retirement accounts, with the help of professionals like estate planners or financial advisors can provide clarity and guidance.

Organizing personal affairs: Amid grief, managing personal matters may feel overwhelming. Organizing essential documents, such as wills, insurance policies, and account information, can help individuals gain control and facilitate the settlement of the deceased's estate. Creating a comprehensive record of assets and liabilities can aid estate administration.

Downsizing and relocating: For some individuals, losing a spouse or loved one may prompt the need to downsize or relocate. This process involves practical considerations, such as deciding on suitable housing options, considering financial implications, and seeking support from real estate professionals or relocation specialists who can assist with the logistics and emotional aspects of the transition.

Estate administration: Settling the deceased's estate can be a complex task. Seeking legal advice and understanding the probate process is essential. Executors or administrators may have responsibilities such as identifying and valuing assets, paying outstanding debts and taxes, and distributing inheritances according to the deceased's wishes.

Subchapter 27.3: Adjusting to a New Normal

<u>Redefining identity and purpose:</u> After losing a spouse or loved one, individuals may experience a shift in their sense of identity and purpose. Exploring personal interests, hobbies, volunteer opportunities, or engaging in meaningful activities can help rediscover a new sense of self and find a renewed purpose in life.

<u>Creating a support system:</u> A solid support system is essential during the transition. Connecting with friends, family, and community resources can provide a sense of belonging and companionship. Seeking professional help, such as grief counseling or therapy, can offer additional support in navigating the emotional challenges and adjusting to the new normal.

<u>Self-care and well-being:</u> Taking care of oneself is crucial during grieving. Practicing self-care activities, such as meditation, mindfulness, or engaging in hobbies, can promote emotional healing and well-being. Prioritizing self-care and setting boundaries can help individuals manage their energy levels and prevent burnout.

<u>Exploring new opportunities:</u> Retirement is a time of exploration and reinvention. After losing a spouse or loved one, individuals may be open to new experiences and opportunities. This may involve pursuing new hobbies, travel, education, or volunteering. Embracing these opportunities can bring joy, fulfillment, and a sense of renewal.

<u>Here are some websites and sources where you can find information about coping with the death of a spouse or loved one in retirement:</u>

- GriefShare (www.griefshare.org): GriefShare is a grief support organization that offers resources, support groups, and educational materials for individuals grieving the loss of a loved one. They provide helpful articles, videos, and tools specifically focused on coping with grief in retirement.
- National Institute on Aging (www.nia.nih.gov): The National

Institute on Aging, a U.S. Department of Health and Human Services division, provides information and resources on various aging-related topics, including grief and bereavement. Their website offers articles, publications, and resources that address coping with the death of a spouse or loved one in retirement.

- Hospice Foundation of America (www.hospicefoundation.org): The Hospice Foundation of America is a nonprofit organization that provides educational resources, support, and programs related to hospice care and end-of-life issues. They have resources specifically focused on grief and loss, including information on coping with the death of a spouse or loved one during retirement.
- AARP (www.aarp.org): AARP offers a wealth of resources for older adults, including information on coping with loss and grief. Their website features articles, guides, and online communities where individuals can find support and advice on navigating the challenges of losing a spouse or loved one in retirement.
- Psychology Today (www.psychologytoday.com): Psychology Today is an online publication covering various mental health topics. They have a dedicated section on grief and bereavement, where you can find articles, expert insights, and resources on coping with loss in retirement.
- Local support groups and counseling services: Besides online resources, consider contacting local support groups, counseling services, or hospice organizations. They may offer grief counseling, bereavement support groups, and other resources specifically tailored to helping individuals cope with losing a spouse or loved one in retirement.

Everyone's grief journey is unique, and finding the support and resources that resonate with your needs is essential. These sources can provide valuable information and guidance, but seeking help from a qualified grief counselor or therapist can also be beneficial in navigating the complex emotions and challenges associated with loss.

Conclusion:

Coping with the death of a spouse or loved one in retirement is a complex and deeply personal journey. This chapter aims to provide comprehensive guidance and support for individuals facing this challenging experience. By understanding the stages of grief, addressing practical considerations, adjusting to a new normal, and seeking help from various sources, individuals can find ways to navigate the grieving process and rebuild their lives with resilience and hope. Everyone's grief journey is unique, and giving oneself time, compassion, and patience is essential as healing occurs.

Chapter 28: Transitioning to Retirement

Transitioning from a career to retirement is a significant life change that requires careful planning and adjustment. In this chapter, we'll explore essential considerations such as choosing an appropriate retirement age, preparing for retirement's psychological and emotional aspects, and strategies for a smooth transition from work to retirement.

Subchapter 28.1: Choosing an Appropriate Retirement Age

Determining the right retirement age is a personal decision that depends on numerous factors, including financial readiness, personal goals, and health considerations. Here are some points to consider when choosing your retirement age:

Financial Readiness: Evaluate your financial situation and determine if you have sufficient savings, investments, and sources of income to support your desired lifestyle throughout retirement. Consult with a financial advisor to assess your financial readiness and determine the ideal retirement age based on your financial goals.

Social Security Benefits: Understand the impact of your retirement age on Social Security benefits. While you can begin receiving reduced benefits as early as sixty-two, waiting until your full retirement age (typically between 66 and 67, depending on your birth year) can result in higher monthly benefit amounts. Delaying benefits further can increase them even more. Consider your Social Security strategy when deciding on your retirement age.

Health and Well-being: Consider your health and energy levels when choosing retirement age. Some individuals may want to retire earlier to enjoy their retirement years while they are still in good health and can pursue their interests and activities. Others may prefer to work longer to maintain social connections, mental stimulation, and a sense of purpose.

Subchapter 28.2: Preparing for the Psychological and Emotional Aspects of Retirement

Retirement involves more than just financial planning; it also requires preparation for this significant life transition's psychological and emotional aspects. Consider the following:

Define Your Purpose: Retirement allows one to explore new passions, hobbies, or volunteer work. Take time to reflect on what gives you a sense of purpose and fulfillment. Consider incorporating these elements into your retirement lifestyle to maintain a sense of meaning and engagement.

Social Connections: Retirees often find their social networks change as they leave the workplace. Proactively cultivate new social connections and maintain existing ones. Consider joining clubs, organizations, or community groups that align with your interests. Staying socially connected is crucial for overall well-being during retirement.

Mental Stimulation: Keep your mind active and engaged by pursuing intellectual activities. This could involve taking classes, attending workshops, reading books, or participating in brain-stimulating games and puzzles. Continued learning and mental stimulation are essential for cognitive health and personal growth.

Emotional Adjustment: Understand that the transition to retirement may bring about a mix of emotions, including excitement, loss, and a sense of identity shift. Give yourself time to adapt to the new lifestyle and be patient with yourself as you navigate this adjustment period. Seek support from loved ones, friends, or professional counselors if needed.

Subchapter 28.3: Strategies for Transitioning from Work to Retirement

Transitioning from work to retirement requires careful planning and adjustment. Here are some strategies to help make the transition smoother:

Gradual Retirement: Consider a phased or gradual retirement approach if it aligns with your circumstances and goals. This involves reducing work hours or taking on part-time or consulting work before fully retiring. Gradual retirement can provide a smoother transition and help bridge the financial gap while allowing you to gradually adjust to a new lifestyle.

Create a Retirement Routine: Establish a daily routine that provides structure and purpose in your retirement. This could involve setting regular times for activities such as exercise, hobbies, social engagements, and personal development. A routine can give your days a sense of direction and help you maintain a healthy and fulfilling lifestyle.

Financial Planning: Review your financial plan and make any necessary adjustments as you transition to retirement. Consider factors such as changes in income, healthcare costs, and potential long-term care needs. Ensure that your budget aligns with your retirement goals and allows for a comfortable and sustainable lifestyle.

Stay Engaged: Seek opportunities to stay engaged with the world around you. This could involve volunteering, joining community organizations, mentoring others, or pursuing part-time work in a field that interests you. Staying engaged can provide a sense of purpose, social interaction, and continued personal growth in retirement.

Manage Your Time: Retirement can bring newfound freedom and flexibility, but managing your time effectively is essential. Prioritize activities that bring you joy and fulfillment while also ensuring you allocate time for relaxation. A balance between productivity and leisure will contribute to a fulfilling retirement lifestyle.

Continual Reflection and Adjustment: Retirement is not a one-time event; it's an ongoing journey. Continually reflect on your retirement experience and make adjustments as needed. Assess whether your retirement goals and aspirations are being met and make necessary changes to align with your evolving priorities and circumstances.

By carefully considering the appropriate retirement age, preparing for the psychological and emotional aspects of retirement, and implementing strategies for a smooth transition from work to retirement, you can confidently navigate this critical life transition and create a fulfilling retirement lifestyle that aligns with your goals and values. Remember to embrace retirement's opportunities and approach this new chapter of life with curiosity, enthusiasm, and a willingness to adapt.

Here are some valuable resources, including websites, books, and other materials, for "Transitioning to Retirement":

Websites:

- AARP (aarp.org): AARP offers many resources for people transitioning into retirement. Their website provides articles, guides, tools, and calculators to help you plan and navigate the retirement transition.
- Retirement Researcher (retirementresearcher.com): This website, run by retirement researcher and author Wade Pfau, provides in-depth analysis and insights into retirement planning. It covers withdrawal strategies, asset allocation, and optimizing Social Security benefits.
- The Balance (thebalance.com): The Balance offers comprehensive guides and articles on retirement planning, including information on transitioning to retirement. You can find tips, checklists, and expert advice to help you navigate this critical life transition.

Books:

- "The New Retirementality: Planning Your Life and Living Your Dreams...at Any Age You Want" by Mitch Anthony: This book explores the non-financial aspects of retirement and helps you redefine retirement based on your personal goals and aspirations.
- "How to Retire Happy, Wild, and Free: Retirement Wisdom That You Won't Get from Your Financial Advisor" by Ernie J. Zelinski: This book offers insights and advice on transitioning to a happy and fulfilling retirement, focusing on lifestyle choices, personal development, and finding purpose.
- "Retirement Reinvention: Make Your Next Act Your Best Act" by Robin Ryan: This book provides strategies and guidance for reinventing your life in retirement, exploring new passions, starting a business, or pursuing meaningful endeavors.

Valuable Resources:

- Retirement Planning Workshops: Many financial institutions and retirement organizations offer workshops or seminars on transitioning to retirement. These events provide valuable information and resources to help you plan and adjust to retirement.
- Retirement Coaches: Consider working with a retirement coach who specializes in helping individuals navigate the transition to retirement. They can provide guidance, support, and customized strategies to help you make the most of this life stage.
- Community Centers and Senior Organizations: Local community centers and senior organizations often offer programs and resources tailored to individuals transitioning into retirement. These resources may include educational workshops, support groups, and social activities.

Remember, transitioning to retirement involves more than just financial planning. It's essential to consider your lifestyle, health, relationships, and personal goals as you navigate this significant life change. Exploring various resources and seeking expert guidance can provide valuable insights and support during this transition period.

Chapter 29: Income Generation in Retirement

Generating income in retirement is crucial to maintain financial stability and support your desired lifestyle. This chapter explores strategies for supplementing retirement income, including part-time work, freelance opportunities, entrepreneurship, and managing income from investments and other sources.

Subchapter 29.1: Supplementing Retirement Income

Supplementing your retirement income can provide financial flexibility and help you achieve your retirement goals. Here are some strategies to consider:

Part-Time Work: Explore part-time job opportunities in your expertise or areas that interest you. Part-time work allows you to stay engaged, maintain a social connection, and earn additional income. Consider flexible work arrangements or consulting opportunities that give you more control over your schedule.

Freelance or Contract Work: Leverage your skills and experience to pursue freelance or contract work. Many industries offer freelance opportunities that allow you to work on a project basis or provide services on a flexible schedule. This can provide an additional source of income while giving you the freedom to choose the projects you enjoy.

Entrepreneurship: Consider starting a small business or pursuing an entrepreneurial venture. This could involve turning a hobby into a business, offering consulting services, or launching an online business. Entrepreneurship can provide financial benefits and a sense of fulfillment and purpose in retirement.

Subchapter 29.2: Managing Income from Investments and Other Sources

Effectively managing income from investments and other sources is essential for a sustainable retirement. Here are some considerations:

Investment Portfolios: Review your investment portfolio and ensure it aligns with your retirement goals. This may involve rebalancing your portfolio to adjust risk levels, exploring income-generating investments such as dividend stocks or bonds, or consulting with a financial advisor to optimize your investment strategy.

Rental Properties: If you own rental properties, they can be a valuable source of income in retirement. Ensure that your parcels are well-maintained, and consider adjusting rental rates periodically to keep up with market trends. If managing properties becomes burdensome, consider hiring a property management company to manage day-to-day operations.

Annuities: Annuities are financial products that provide regular income in retirement. They can be purchased from insurance companies and offer diverse options, such as fixed or variable annuities. Consider consulting with a financial advisor to determine if an annuity aligns with your financial goals and risk tolerance.

Social Security and Pension Benefits: Maximize your Social Security benefits by carefully considering the best time to start receiving them. Delaying benefits beyond your full retirement age can result in higher monthly payments. If you have a pension, understand the payout options and consider the best strategy for claiming those benefits.

Rental Income: If you have unused space in your home, consider renting it out as an additional source of income. This could involve renting a room through platforms like Airbnb or finding long-term tenants. Ensure you comply with local regulations and take the necessary steps to protect your property and privacy.

Dividends and Interest: If you invest in stocks, bonds, or savings accounts, dividends and interest can provide a steady income stream. Regularly review your investments and consider reinvesting the income or using it to cover your expenses.

Regularly review your income sources, adjust your strategies as needed, and consult with financial professionals to ensure your income generation plan aligns with your retirement goals and circumstances. By supplementing your retirement income through part-time work, freelance opportunities, or entrepreneurship and effectively managing income from investments and other sources, you can enhance your retirement financial security and maintain a comfortable lifestyle. Here are some additional points to consider:

Budgeting and Cash Flow Management: Develop a comprehensive budget that accounts for your retirement income and expenses. Track your cash flow to ensure you clearly understand your financial situation. Identify areas where you can reduce costs or optimize spending to maximize your retirement income.

Tax Considerations: Understand the tax implications of your income sources in retirement. Some income may be subject to taxes, while others may have tax advantages. Consult with a tax advisor to explore strategies for minimizing tax liability and maximizing your after-tax income.

Diversification: Diversify your income sources to mitigate risk and increase financial stability. Relying on a sole source of income may leave you vulnerable to economic fluctuations. You can create a more resilient financial foundation by diversifying your income streams, such as combining part-time work with investment income, rental income, or other sources.

Longevity Planning: Consider the potential length of your retirement and plan accordingly. Ensuring your income sources can sustain you throughout your retirement years is essential with increasing life expectancy. Account for inflation and unexpected expenses when determining your income generation strategy.

Ongoing Evaluation: Regularly review and evaluate your income generation strategy. Monitor the performance of your investments, reassess your budget, and adjust your approach as needed. Stay informed about market trends, economic changes, and new income opportunities that may arise.

Seek Professional Guidance: If you need clarification on the best retirement income generation strategies, consider collaborating with a financial advisor or specialist. They can provide personalized guidance based on your specific circumstances and help you navigate the complexities of managing income in retirement.

By exploring opportunities for supplementing retirement income through part-time work, freelance opportunities, or entrepreneurship and effectively managing income from investments and other sources, you can enhance your financial security, maintain a comfortable lifestyle, and enjoy a fulfilling retirement journey. Every individual's financial situation is unique, so it's essential to tailor your income generation strategies to your specific needs and goals.

Here are some valuable resources, including websites, books, and other materials, for "Income Generation in Retirement":

Websites:

- Investopedia (investopedia.com): Investopedia offers comprehensive articles and guides on various investment strategies and income generation options for retirees. You can find information on dividend investing, real estate investment, and annuities.
- Bogleheads (bogleheads.org): Bogleheads is a community of investors who follow the principles of John C. Bogle, the founder of Vanguard. Their forum and wiki provide insights and discussions on retirement income strategies, including

portfolio construction, asset allocation, and withdrawal strategies.

- Social Security Administration (ssa.gov): The official website of the Social Security Administration provides detailed information on Social Security benefits, including retirement benefits, spousal benefits, and survivor benefits. You can use their calculators and tools to estimate benefits and explore different claiming strategies.

<u>Books:</u>

- "The Ultimate Retirement Guide for 50+: Winning Strategies to Make Your Money Last a Lifetime" by Suze Orman: This book offers advice on retirement income planning, including strategies for maximizing Social Security benefits, managing investment portfolios, and generating income in retirement.
- "The Bogleheads' Guide to Retirement Planning" by Taylor Larimore, Mel Lindauer, and Richard A. Ferri: This book provides a comprehensive guide to retirement planning, covering topics such as investment strategies, tax planning, and creating a sustainable retirement income stream.
- "Get What's Yours: The Secrets to Maxing Out Your Social Security" by Laurence J. Kotlikoff, Philip Moeller, and Paul Solman: This book focuses on maximizing Social Security benefits and navigating the complexities of the system to ensure you receive the highest possible income in retirement.

<u>Valuable Resources:</u>

- Financial Advisors and Planners: Collaborating with a qualified financial advisor or planner can help you develop a customized retirement income strategy based on your goals, risk tolerance, and financial situation. They can provide insights into investment options, tax-efficient withdrawal strategies, and overall retirement planning.

- Retirement Income Calculators: Several online calculators can help you estimate your retirement income needs and explore different scenarios. Tools like the Vanguard Retirement Income Calculator, Fidelity Retirement Income Planner, and T. Rowe Price Retirement Income Calculator can assist you in evaluating different income generation strategies.

- Dividend Investing Websites: If you're interested in generating income through dividend investing, websites like Dividend.com and Seeking Alpha's Dividend Strategy section provide resources, articles, and stock screeners to help you identify dividend-paying stocks and build a dividend portfolio.

Remember, generating income in retirement requires careful planning and consideration of numerous factors, such as your risk tolerance, income needs, and tax implications. Assessing your circumstances and consulting financial professionals to create a strategy that aligns with your goals and objectives is essential.

Chapter 30: Running A Business In Retirement

Running a business in retirement can be an exciting and fulfilling endeavor. It provides an opportunity to pursue a passion, stay engaged, generate income, and maintain a sense of purpose during retirement. This chapter will explore the various aspects of running a business in retirement, including real-world scenarios, advice, tips, and tricks to help you succeed.

Subchapter 30.1: Choosing the Right Business

When considering running a business in retirement, choosing a venture that aligns with your interests, skills, and experience is essential. Here are some considerations to keep in mind:

1. Assess your skills and passions: Reflect on your expertise, hobbies, and interests. What skills do you possess that could be turned into a business? What activities bring you joy and fulfillment?
2. Research the market: Conduct market research to identify potential business opportunities. Look for gaps or underserved niches in the market that align with your skills and interests.
3. Consider your resources: Evaluate the financial and time resources you can allocate to the business. Determine how much capital you're willing to invest and how much time you can spend.
4. Seek advice and mentorship: Consult with business professionals or mentors who can provide guidance and insights based on their experience. They can help you assess the feasibility of your business idea and provide valuable

advice.

Subchapter 30.2: Developing a Business Plan

A well-thought-out business plan is crucial for the success of your venture. It serves as a roadmap, guiding your decisions and actions. Consider the following elements when developing your business plan:

1. Executive summary: Provide an overview of your business, including its mission, vision, and objectives.
2. Market analysis: Conduct thorough research of your target market, including customer demographics, competitors, and market trends.
3. Products and services: Clearly define the products or services you will offer and explain how they meet the needs of your target market.
4. Marketing and sales strategies: Outline your marketing and sales tactics, including pricing, promotion, and distribution channels.
5. Operations and management: Describe the operational aspects of your business, such as location, staffing, and processes.

1. Financial projections: Develop financial forecasts, including projected revenue, expenses, and profitability. Consider factors such as startup costs, ongoing fees, and pricing strategies.

Subchapter 30.3: Legal and Regulatory Considerations

Running a business in retirement involves complying with various legal and regulatory requirements. Here are some key considerations:

1. Business structure: Choose an appropriate legal structure for your business, such as a sole proprietorship, partnership, or limited liability company (LLC). Consult with a legal professional or accountant to understand the implications of each structure.

2. Licensing and permits: Determine if your business requires any specific licenses or permits to operate legally. Research the requirements at the local, state, and federal levels.

3. Tax obligations: Understand the tax obligations of running a business. Consult with a tax advisor to ensure tax law compliance and maximize tax benefits.

4. Insurance coverage: Evaluate the insurance needs of your business, such as general liability insurance, professional liability insurance, or product liability insurance. Obtain appropriate coverage to protect your business and personal assets.

Subchapter 30.4: Managing Finances and Cash Flow

Proper fiscal management is critical for the success and sustainability of your business. Consider the following tips:

1. Separate personal and business finances: Open a separate bank account for your business to maintain a clear separation between personal and business expenses.

2. Budgeting and forecasting: Develop a budget and regularly review your financial performance. Forecast your cash flow to anticipate any potential shortfalls or surpluses.

3. Pricing strategies: Set prices that reflect the value of your products or services and cover your costs. Consider competitors' pricing, market demand, and profit margins.

4. Cash flow management: Monitor your cash flow closely to

ensure you have sufficient funds to cover expenses, pay suppliers, and reinvest in your business. Implement strategies to manage cash flow, such as offering discounts for early payments or negotiating favorable payment terms with suppliers.

Subchapter 30.5: Marketing and Customer Acquisition

Effective marketing is crucial for attracting and retaining customers. Consider the following strategies:

1. Define your target audience: Identify your ideal customers based on demographics, interests, and needs. Tailor your marketing efforts to reach and engage this specific audience.

1. Build an online presence: Create a professional website and utilize social media platforms to showcase your products or services. Engage with potential customers through informative content, promotions, and customer testimonials.
2. Networking and partnerships: Attend industry events, join local business associations, and network with other professionals. Establish partnerships with complementary businesses to expand your reach and leverage shared audiences.
3. Customer relationship management: Focus on building solid customer relationships. Provide excellent customer service, seek feedback, and implement strategies to encourage repeat business and referrals.

Subchapter 30.6: Balancing Retirement and Business

Running a business in retirement requires finding a balance between work and personal life. Consider these tips for achieving harmony:

1. Set clear boundaries: Establish specific working hours and boundaries to separate work time from personal time. Stick to these boundaries to avoid burnout and maintain a healthy work-life balance.

2. Delegate and outsource: Identify tasks that can be delegated or outsourced to free up your time and focus on core business activities. Consider hiring part-time employees, virtual assistants, or freelancers to manage non-essential tasks.

3. Prioritize self-care: Take care of your physical and mental well-being. Engage in activities that bring you joy and relaxation outside of work. Prioritize exercise, healthy eating, and sufficient rest to maintain overall well-being.

4. Plan for retirement savings: While running a business in retirement can provide income, ensure that you continue to save for retirement. Consult with a financial advisor to develop retirement savings plan those accounts for both business income and personal protection.

Here are some websites and resources where you can find more information on running a business in retirement:

-   Small Business Administration (SBA) - The SBA provides resources, guides, and information on starting and managing a small business. Visit their website at www.sba.gov.
-   SCORE - SCORE is a nonprofit organization that offers free mentoring, resources, and workshops to small business owners and entrepreneurs. They have a specific section

dedicated to retirement-age entrepreneurs. Explore their website at www.score.org.

- AARP - AARP offers a wealth of information and resources for individuals aged fifty and older. They have a section on their website dedicated to starting and running a business in retirement. Visit their website at www.aarp.org.

- U.S. Chamber of Commerce - The U.S. Chamber of Commerce provides valuable resources, guides, and tools for small business owners. Their website, www.uschamber.com, offers insights and information on running a business.

- Entrepreneur - Entrepreneur is a well-known publication that covers assorted topics related to entrepreneurship and small business management. Their website, www.entrepreneur.com, provides articles, guides, and expert advice on starting and running a business.

- Inc. - Inc. is another reputable publication focusing on startups and small business success. Their website, www.inc.com, features articles, resources, and insights for entrepreneurs.

- Small Business Development Centers (SBDC) - SBDCs are a network of centers across the United States that provide free or low-cost consulting services, training programs, and resources to small business owners. Locate your nearest SBDC and access their services by visiting www.sba.gov/local-assistance/find.

- Business.gov - Business.gov is a comprehensive resource for small business owners, providing information on legal requirements, licenses, permits, and regulations. Explore their website at www.business.gov.

- Local Chambers of Commerce - Check your local Chamber of Commerce website for resources, networking opportunities, and support for small business owners. They often provide guidance specific to your local area.

Remember to use these resources as starting points for your research. Each website offers a wealth of information and may lead you to further resources, guides, and tools to help you succeed in running a business in retirement.

Conclusion:

Running a business in retirement can be a fulfilling and financially rewarding venture. You can increase your chances of success by carefully selecting the right company, developing a comprehensive business plan, adhering to legal and regulatory requirements, managing finances effectively, implementing robust marketing strategies, and maintaining a healthy work-life balance. Remember, running a business in retirement should be an enjoyable and purposeful endeavor, allowing you to continue to grow, contribute, and thrive during this phase of life.

Chapter 31: Understanding Pension Benefits in Retirement

Retirement is a significant phase in one's life, marking the transition from a career-oriented lifestyle to a period of leisure and relaxation. During retirement, it becomes crucial to have a stable and reliable source of income to sustain one's desired standard of living. This is where pension benefits play a vital role.

Pension benefits are a form of retirement income employers, or government entities provide to eligible individuals. These benefits ensure financial security during retirement by providing a steady income stream after an individual stops working. They serve as a reward for years of service and dedication to a particular employer or as a social security measure provided by the government.

The primary purpose of pension benefits is to replace a portion of the individual's pre-retirement income, enabling them to maintain their lifestyle and meet their financial obligations even after leaving the workforce. Understanding how pension benefits work and the several types available is essential for effective retirement planning.

Pensions can come in different forms, but the two main types are defined benefit and contribution pension plans.

Defined benefit pension plans are traditional employer-sponsored plans that guarantee a specific benefit amount based on a predetermined formula. This formula often considers factors such as years of service and salary history. With a defined benefit plan, the employer assumes the investment risk and funds the plan. This means the employer must provide the specified benefit amount to the retiree, regardless of the plan's investment performance.

On the other hand, defined contribution pension plans shift the investment risk and responsibility to the employee. In these plans, employees contribute a portion of their salary into individual accounts, and employers may match a percentage of these contributions. The accumulated funds are then invested in various investment options the employee chooses, such as mutual funds or stocks. The total contributions, investment returns, and the performance of the chosen investments determine the ultimate retirement benefit in a defined contribution plan.

It is important to note that pension benefits are subject to eligibility criteria and vesting requirements. Eligibility criteria vary depending on the type of pension plan and the specific rules set by the employer or government entity. Generally, an individual must fulfill particular service requirements, such as working for a specified number of years, to become eligible for pension benefits.

Vesting refers to the employee's right to the employer's contributions to their pension plan. While employee contributions are usually fully vested, employer contributions may be subject to a vesting schedule. A vesting schedule determines how long an employee must work for the employer before they are entitled to the employer's contributions. Understanding the vesting schedule is crucial, as it determines how much of the employer's contributions an employee can take with them if they leave the job before retirement.

In conclusion, pension benefits are a crucial component of retirement planning. They provide a steady income stream during retirement, ensuring financial security and maintaining one's desired lifestyle. Understanding the several types of pension plans, eligibility criteria, vesting requirements, and income options is essential for making informed decisions and maximizing pension benefits. By carefully considering pension options, saving and investing in additional retirement accounts, and staying knowledgeable about changes to pension plans, individuals can enhance their financial security and enjoy a comfortable retirement.

Subchapter 31.1: Types of Pensions

Defined Benefit Pension Plans

Defined benefit pension plans are traditional employer-sponsored plans that guarantee a specific benefit amount based on a formula, often linked to years of service and salary history. With a defined benefit plan, the employer assumes the investment risk and funds the plan. The benefit amount is typically calculated as a percentage of the average salary during the highest earning years.

For example, let's consider John, who has worked for a company for 30 years. His defined benefit plan promises him 2% of his average salary during his last five years of employment for each year of service. If his average wage in the previous five years is $80,000, his annual pension benefit would be $48,000 (2% x 30 years x $80,000).

Defined Contribution Pension Plans

Defined contribution pension plans, such as 401(k)s and individual retirement accounts (IRAs), are becoming more prevalent in today's workforce. Unlike defined benefit plans, the benefit amount in defined contribution plans depends on the contributions made and investment returns.

In these plans, employees contribute a portion of their salary into individual accounts, and employers may match a percentage of these contributions. The accumulated funds are invested, often in a selection of mutual funds or other investment options chosen by the employee. Upon retirement, the individual receives the accumulated balance in their account.

For example, Sarah participates in a 401(k)-plan offered by her employer. She contributes 5% of her $50,000 annual salary, and her employer matches 50% of her contributions. Over 30 years, assuming an average annual return of 7%, her 401(k) balance could grow to approximately $570,000.

Subchapter 31.2: Eligibility and Vesting

<u>Eligibility Criteria</u>

Eligibility criteria for pension benefits vary depending on the type of plan and the employer. Defined benefit plans often require a minimum number of years of service, such as five or ten years, before an employee becomes eligible for benefits. On the other hand, defined contribution plans typically allow immediate participation without a service requirement.

Additionally, some pension plans have age requirements, such as age 55 or 65, to qualify for full benefits. It's essential to review your employer's pension plan documents or consult with the human resources department to understand the specific eligibility criteria for your plan.

<u>Vesting</u>

Vesting refers to the employee's right to the employer's contributions to their pension plan. In defined contribution plans, employee contributions are always 100% vested, meaning they have ownership of their contributions and any associated earnings. However, employer contributions may be subject to a vesting schedule.

A vesting schedule determines how long an employee must work for the employer before they are entitled to the employer's contributions. Standard vesting schedules include three- or five-year cliff vesting or graded vesting, where a certain percentage of employer contributions becomes vested each year. Understanding your plan's vesting schedule is crucial to determine how much of the employer's contributions you are entitled to if you leave your job before retirement.

Subchapter 31.3: Maximizing Pension Benefits

<u>Pension Income Options</u>

When you retire and start receiving pension benefits, you'll typically have different income options. Common options include:

Single-life annuity: This option provides a monthly income for your lifetime but ends when you pass away. It is suitable for individuals who don't have dependents or have other sources of income for their beneficiaries.

Joint and survivor annuity: With this option, you receive a reduced monthly income, but if you pass away, your surviving spouse or beneficiary continues to receive a portion of the benefit for their lifetime. It ensures financial security for your spouse or dependent.

Lump sum distribution: Instead of receiving monthly payments, you may have the option to take a lump sum distribution. This provides a one-time fee, which you can invest or use as needed. However, evaluating the tax implications and potential investment risks is crucial before choosing this option.

<u>Pension Maximization Strategies</u>

If you have a defined benefit pension plan and are offered a choice between a higher pension benefit or a lump sum distribution, you may consider pension maximization strategies. These strategies involve taking the higher pension benefit and purchasing life insurance to provide a death benefit for your spouse or beneficiaries.

By selecting the higher pension benefit, you receive a more considerable monthly income during your lifetime. Simultaneously, the life insurance policy can replace the reduced survivor benefit for your spouse or beneficiaries if you pass away. However, pension maximization strategies can be complex, and it's essential to consult a financial advisor to evaluate the suitability and potential risks involved.

Subchapter 31.4: Tips and Tricks for Pension Planning

<u>Start Planning Early</u>

The key to maximizing your pension benefits is planning as early as possible. Understand your pension plan options and make informed decisions based on your financial goals and circumstances. The more time you have to contribute to a defined contribution plan or accumulate years of service in a defined benefit plan, the better your retirement income will be.

<u>Save and Invest in Additional Retirement Accounts</u>

While pension benefits provide a valuable source of retirement income, it's wise to supplement them with additional savings and investments. Contribute to individual retirement accounts (IRAs) or other retirement vehicles to take advantage of tax benefits and build a diverse retirement portfolio. Consider collaborating with a financial advisor to develop a comprehensive retirement savings strategy.

<u>Stay Informed and Monitor Your Pension Plan</u>

Pension plans can change, including adjustments to benefit formulas, contribution levels, or plan provisions. Stay informed about any updates or modifications to your pension plan and how they may impact your retirement income. Regularly review your plan statements, investment options, and beneficiary designations to ensure they align with your goals.

<u>Here are some websites and valuable resources that provide further assistance and knowledge regarding pension benefits and retirement planning:</u>

- Pension Rights Center (www.pensionrights.org): The Pension Rights Center is a nonprofit organization that offers a wealth of information and resources on pension rights, including publications, fact sheets, and tools for understanding and navigating pension plans.
- U.S. Department of Labor - Employee Benefits Security

Administration (www.dol.gov/agencies/ebsa): The Employee Benefits Security Administration (EBSA) is a division of the U.S. Department of Labor that provides information and resources on pension plans, retirement benefits, and employee rights. Their website offers comprehensive guides, publications, and tools to help individuals understand their pension benefits.

- Social Security Administration (www.ssa.gov): The Social Security Administration website is invaluable for understanding Social Security benefits and retirement planning. It provides information on eligibility, benefit calculations, and various retirement benefit options.
- Financial Industry Regulatory Authority (FINRA) (www.finra.org): FINRA offers a range of educational resources and tools to help individuals make informed financial decisions. Their website provides information on retirement planning, including retirement calculators, guides, and investor alerts to navigate the complexities of retirement planning and pension benefits.
- AARP (www.aarp.org): AARP is an organization dedicated to empowering and supporting older adults. Their website offers a variety of resources, articles, and tools related to retirement planning, including pension benefits, Social Security, and other aspects of retirement income.
- The Pensions Advisory Service (www.pensionsadvisoryservice.org.uk): For individuals in the United Kingdom, The Pensions Advisory Service is an excellent resource. It provides free and impartial guidance on pension matters, including information on several types of pensions, retirement planning, and understanding pension benefits.
- Retirement Planning Tools and Calculators: Many financial

institutions and websites offer retirement planning tools and calculators. These tools can help individuals estimate their future pension benefits, plan for retirement, and explore different scenarios. Some examples include Fidelity's Retirement Income Planner (www.fidelity.com/calculators-tools/retirement-income-planner) and Vanguard's Retirement Nest Egg Calculator (www.vanguard.com/nesteggcalculator).

Remember, it's always advisable to consult with financial advisors, retirement planning professionals, or pension specialists who can provide personalized guidance based on your situation and goals.

<u>Conclusion</u>

Understanding pension benefits is essential for a successful retirement plan. Whether you have a defined benefit plan or a defined contribution plan, knowing the eligibility criteria, vesting requirements, and income options will help you make informed decisions. By maximizing your pension benefits through careful planning, considering different strategies, and supplementing with additional retirement savings, you can enhance your financial security and enjoy a comfortable retirement.

Chapter 32: Annuities; How They Work in Retirement

As individuals approach retirement, one of the critical considerations is ensuring a steady and reliable income stream during their post-work years. Annuities are financial products specifically designed to address this need. In this chapter, we will explore the ins and outs of annuities, how they work in retirement, and their pros and cons.

An annuity is a contract between an individual, known as the annuitant, and an insurance company. It is an investment vehicle that provides regular income payments to the annuitant for a specified period or the rest of their life. Annuities can be purchased through a lump sum or a series of payments over time.

Subchapter 32.1: Types of Annuities

Fixed Annuities

Fixed annuities are the most straightforward type of annuity. With a fixed annuity, the insurance company guarantees a fixed rate of return on the invested principal. This means that the annuitant will receive a predetermined amount of income during the annuity's payout phase.

For example, consider Mary, who purchases a fixed annuity with a principal of $100,000 and a guaranteed annual interest rate of 4%. In this scenario, Mary will receive $4,000 annually as income from the annuity. The payment amount remains the same regardless of the performance of the underlying investments.

Variable Annuities

As the name suggests, variable annuities offer more flexibility and potential for growth than fixed annuities. With variable annuities, the annuitant can invest their principal in various sub-accounts, similar to mutual funds. The performance of these sub-accounts determines the value and income of the grant.

Variable annuities provide the opportunity for higher returns, as the investment performance directly impacts the income payments. However, this also means that the annuitant bears the investment risk. If the sub-accounts perform well, the income payments may stay the same.

Immediate Annuities

Immediate annuities are purchased with a lump sum payment and begin providing income payments immediately or shortly after the purchase. They are suitable for individuals who need a regular income stream as soon as possible in retirement. The income from an immediate annuity is determined by factors such as the principal amount, the annuitant's life expectancy, and prevailing interest rates.

For example, John retires and invests $200,000 in an immediate annuity. Based on his age and life expectancy, the insurance company determines he will receive $1,500 monthly for the rest of his life. This provides John with a predictable and stable income throughout retirement.

Deferred Annuities

Deferred annuities are designed to provide income at a later date, allowing individuals to accumulate funds over a specified period before starting the payout phase. During the accumulation phase, the principal grows tax-deferred, meaning taxes on investment gains are deferred until withdrawal.

Deferred annuities offer more flexibility in terms of contribution amounts and timing. Individuals can contribute to the annuity periodically or make a lump sum payment. The annuity's value grows over time based on the performance of the underlying investments.

For example, Sarah is in her forties and wants to supplement her retirement savings. She decides to invest $10,000 annually in a deferred annuity until she reaches retirement age at 65. The annuity grows tax-deferred, and when Sarah retires, she can choose various payout options, such as a lump sum, regular income payments, or a combination of both.

Subchapter 32.2: Annuity Payout Options

<u>Immediate Annuities</u>

Immediate annuities are purchased with a lump sum payment and begin providing income payments immediately or shortly after the purchase. They are suitable for individuals who need a regular income stream as soon as possible in retirement. The income from an immediate annuity is determined by factors such as the principal amount, the annuitant's life expectancy, and prevailing interest rates.

For example, John retires and invests $200,000 in an immediate annuity. Based on his age and life expectancy, the insurance company determines he will receive $1,500 monthly for the rest of his life. This provides John with a predictable and stable income throughout retirement.

Deferred Annuities

Deferred annuities are designed to provide income at a later date, allowing individuals to accumulate funds over a specified period before starting the payout phase. During the accumulation phase, the principal grows tax-deferred, meaning taxes on investment gains are deferred until withdrawal.

Deferred annuities offer more flexibility in terms of contribution amounts and timing. Individuals can contribute to the annuity periodically or make a lump sum payment. The annuity's value grows over time based on the performance of the underlying investments.

For example, Sarah is in her forties and wants to supplement her retirement savings. She decides to invest $10,000 annually in a deferred annuity until she reaches retirement age at 65. The annuity grows tax-deferred, and when Sarah retires, she can choose various payout options, such as a lump sum, regular income payments, or a combination of both.

Subchapter 32.3: Pros and Cons of Annuities

<u>Pros of Annuities</u>

Guaranteed Income: Annuities provide a guaranteed income stream, which can help individuals meet their financial needs and maintain their desired standard of living during retirement.

Tax Advantages: Annuities offer tax-deferred growth, meaning the investment gains are not taxed until withdrawal. This allows the principal to grow faster over time.

Flexibility: Annuities come with various payout options, allowing individuals to customize their income stream based on their unique preferences and financial goals.

<u>Cons of Annuities</u>

Lack of Liquidity: Annuities are long-term commitments, and accessing the principal can be challenging. Early withdrawals may result in surrender charges or penalties, and surrendering the annuity altogether may incur significant fees.

Complexity and Fees: Annuities can be complex financial products with various fees, such as administrative fees, mortality and expense fees, and investment management fees. It is essential to carefully review and understand the costs associated with an annuity before purchasing.

Inflation Risk: Fixed annuities may not keep pace with inflation, meaning the purchasing power of the income payments may decrease over time.

Subchapter 32.4: Tips and Tricks for Annuity Selection

Assess Your Needs: Before purchasing an annuity, assess your financial goals, risk tolerance, and income needs in retirement. This will help determine the type of annuity that best aligns with your circumstances.

Shop Around: Annuity contracts vary significantly regarding fees, features, and benefits. Take the time to shop around, compare offerings from different insurance companies, and seek professional advice to find the most suitable annuity for your needs.

Understand the Fine Print: Carefully read and understand the terms and conditions of the annuity contract. Pay attention to fees, surrender charges, and applicable limitations or restrictions.

Here are some websites and valuable resources that provide further assistance and knowledge regarding annuities and retirement planning:

- The American Association of Retired Persons (AARP) (www.aarp.org): AARP is an organization dedicated to empowering and supporting older adults. Their website offers a variety of resources, articles, and tools related to annuities, retirement planning, and other aspects of retirement income.
- Financial Industry Regulatory Authority (FINRA) (www.finra.org): FINRA offers a range of educational resources and tools to help individuals make informed financial decisions. Their website provides information on annuities, retirement planning, and investor alerts to navigate the complexities of financial products and retirement income.
- U.S. Securities and Exchange Commission (SEC) - Annuities (www.sec.gov/reportspubs/investor-publications/ investorpubsannuityhtm.html): The SEC provides an investor publication specifically focused on annuities. It covers essential topics such as types of annuities, risks, fees, and tips for evaluating and purchasing annuities.
- National Association of Insurance Commissioners (NAIC) (www.naic.org): The NAIC website offers resources and guides on annuities, including consumer information and tools to help individuals understand and compare annuity products.
- Pension Rights Center (www.pensionrights.org): The Pension Rights Center provides resources and information

on retirement income, including annuities. Their website offers publications, fact sheets, and tools for understanding and navigating annuity products and retirement planning.

- U.S. Department of Labor - Employee Benefits Security Administration (www.dol.gov/agencies/ebsa): The Employee Benefits Security Administration (EBSA) is a division of the U.S. Department of Labor that provides information and resources on retirement benefits, including annuities. Their website offers guides, publications, and tools to help individuals understand annuities and make informed decisions.

- Retirement Planning Tools and Calculators: Many financial institutions and retirement planning websites offer tools and calculators specifically for annuities. These tools can help individuals estimate their potential annuity income, compare different annuity options, and explore various scenarios. Examples include Fidelity's Annuity Calculator (www.fidelity.com/calculators-tools/annuity-calculator) and Vanguard's Annuity Payout Calculator (www.vanguard.com/calculators/annuity-payout).

Remember, it's always advisable to consult with financial advisors, retirement planning professionals, or insurance specialists who can provide personalized guidance based on your situation and goals. These resources can be a starting point for gathering information and understanding annuities, but professional advice is crucial for making well-informed decisions.

<u>Conclusion</u>

Annuities can be valuable financial tools for creating a reliable income stream during retirement. They offer the assurance of guaranteed income, tax advantages, and flexibility in payout options. However, it is essential to consider the pros and cons of annuities and evaluate them in the context of your specific financial goals and circumstances.

Individuals can make informed decisions when incorporating annuities into their retirement planning strategy by understanding the several types of annuities and payout options and considering factors such as liquidity, fees, and inflation risk. Consulting with financial advisors or retirement planning professionals can provide personalized guidance and help navigate the complexities of annuities to ensure they align with your long-term financial objectives.

Chapter 33: How To Reinvest In Retirement

As individuals enter retirement, their financial goals and investment strategies may shift. Reinvesting in retirement refers to managing and allocating funds to generate income, preserve capital, and meet financial objectives. This chapter will explore various strategies and real-world scenarios and provide advice and tips on reinvesting effectively during retirement.

Subchapter 33.1: Assessing Retirement Goals and Risk Tolerance

Before diving into reinvestment strategies, it is essential to reassess your retirement goals and risk tolerance. Consider desired income, lifestyle, legacy planning, and time horizon. Also, evaluate your risk tolerance, which may change as you retire. Understanding your goals and risk tolerance will help guide your reinvestment decisions.

Subchapter 33.2: Diversification and Asset Allocation

Diversification:

Diversification is a fundamental principle of investing that involves spreading your investments across different asset classes, such as stocks, bonds, real estate, and cash equivalents. By diversifying, you reduce the risk associated with a concentrated portfolio. Diversification allows you to participate in various market segments, potentially mitigating losses in one area with gains in another.

For example, let's consider Patricia, who recently retired. She diversifies her portfolio by allocating some of her retirement savings to stocks, bonds, and real estate investment trusts (REITs). This approach helps Patricia minimize the impact of a downturn in one asset class.

<u>Asset Allocation:</u>

Asset allocation refers to the strategic distribution of investments among different asset classes based on your risk tolerance, time horizon, and financial goals. It involves determining the appropriate mix of stocks, bonds, and other assets to achieve the desired balance between growth and income.

For instance, Mark wants a balanced approach to reinvesting his retirement funds. Based on his risk tolerance and financial goals, he allocates 60% of his portfolio to stocks for growth potential and 40% to bonds for income and stability.

Subchapter 33.3: Income-Generating Strategies

Dividend-Paying Stocks:

Dividend-paying stocks can provide a steady income stream during retirement. These are stocks issued by companies that distribute a portion of their profits to shareholders as dividends. Investing in established companies with a history of consistent dividend payments can be an attractive option for retirees seeking income.

For example, Susan allocates a portion of her retirement portfolio to dividend-paying stocks. She selects companies with a history of increasing dividend payouts over time, providing her with a reliable income source.

Bonds and Fixed-Income Investments:

Bonds and fixed-income investments are popular choices for retirees seeking stable income. These investments provide regular interest payments and a return of principal upon maturity. Government bonds, corporate bonds, and bond funds offer varying yields and risk profiles, allowing retirees to tailor their investments to their risk tolerance.

Example: John decides to allocate some of his retirement savings to a bond portfolio consisting of government and high-quality corporate bonds. This helps him generate a predictable income stream and preserve his capital.

Subchapter 33.4: Managing Risk and Volatility

Risk Management:

Retirees should be mindful of managing risk in their investment portfolios. Strategies such as diversification, asset allocation, and periodic portfolio rebalancing can help mitigate risk. Reviewing and adjusting your investments periodically to ensure they align with your risk tolerance and financial goals is essential.

Managing Market Volatility:

Retirees may face market volatility during their retirement years. It is crucial to remain calm and avoid making impulsive investment decisions based on short-term market fluctuations. Long-term investment plans should be based on your financial goals and time horizon. Consult with a financial advisor who can guide volatile market conditions.

Subchapter 33.5: Seeking Professional Guidance

Financial Advisor:

Retirees can benefit from collaborating with a financial advisor specializing in retirement planning. An advisor can help develop a comprehensive investment strategy, provide ongoing guidance, and monitor your portfolio's performance. They can also assist with tax planning, estate planning, and other financial aspects of retirement.

Continuing Education:

Retirement planning is an ongoing process, and staying informed about current market trends, investment strategies, and retirement-related topics is essential. Attend seminars, workshops, or webinars hosted by reputable financial institutions or organizations to expand your knowledge and make informed investment decisions.

Here are some websites and valuable resources that provide further assistance and knowledge for retirement planning and reinvesting:

- The U.S. Securities and Exchange Commission (SEC) - Retirement: The SEC's website offers a dedicated section on retirement planning, including resources on investment strategies, managing risk, and investor alerts. It provides valuable information to help individuals make informed decisions during retirement. (www.sec.gov/retirement)
- The Financial Industry Regulatory Authority (FINRA) - Retirement Planning: FINRA offers a range of educational resources on retirement planning, including information on investing, managing risk, and avoiding scams. Their website provides tools, calculators, and publications to help individuals plan for retirement. (www.finra.org/investors/retirement-planning)
- The National Institute on Retirement Security (NIRS): NIRS is a non-profit research and education organization focused on retirement security. Their website offers research reports, policy briefs, and resources related to retirement planning and investment strategies. (www.nirsonline.org)
- The Employee Benefit Research Institute (EBRI): EBRI researches retirement and employee benefits. Their website provides access to publications, research papers, and data on retirement planning, savings, and investment trends. (www.ebri.org)
- The American Association of Retired Persons (AARP) - Money and Retirement: AARP offers a wealth of information on retirement planning, investment strategies, and financial security. Their website provides articles, guides,

and tools to help individuals navigate the various aspects of retirement. (www.aarp.org/money/)

- The Vanguard Group - Retirement Planning: Vanguard, an investment management company, offers a comprehensive retirement planning section on its website. It provides resources, tools, and calculators to help individuals plan, save, and invest for retirement. (investor.vanguard.com/retirement/)

- The Fidelity Investments - Retirement Planning: Fidelity is another well-known investment company that provides a wide range of retirement planning resources. Their website offers articles, videos, retirement calculators, and tools to help individuals make informed investment decisions. (www.fidelity.com/retirement- planning/overview)

- The Charles Schwab - Retirement Planning Center: Charles Schwab's Retirement Planning Center provides educational content, tools, and resources to help individuals with retirement planning and investment strategies. Their website offers articles, guides, and retirement calculators. (www.schwab.com/retirement-planning)

Remember, while these resources can provide valuable information and guidance, it's always advisable to consult with a financial advisor or retirement planning professional who can provide personalized advice based on your financial situation and goals.

Conclusion:

Reinvesting in retirement involves careful consideration of goals, risk tolerance, diversification, and income-generating strategies. You can create a sustainable investment plan that aligns with your retirement needs by reassessing your objectives, diversifying your portfolio, and seeking professional guidance. Stay informed, adapt to changing market conditions, and periodically review your investment strategy to ensure it aligns with your goals and risk tolerance throughout your retirement journey.

Chapter 34: Longevity and Healthcare Considerations

As you plan for retirement, it's essential to consider the potential impact of longevity and healthcare expenses. This chapter will explore strategies for managing longevity risk, maintaining health and wellness in retirement, and addressing potential healthcare challenges.

Subchapter 34.1: Strategies for Managing Longevity Risk

Longevity risk refers to the possibility of outliving your retirement savings. To manage this risk effectively, consider the following strategies:

Financial Planning: Assess your financial situation and project your retirement expenses based on a longer life expectancy. Work with a financial advisor to develop a comprehensive retirement plan those accounts for potential healthcare costs, inflation, and other factors. Consider strategies such as delaying Social Security benefits, maximizing retirement account contributions, and exploring guaranteed income options like annuities.

Long-Term Care Insurance: Long-term care insurance can help protect your savings from the potentially inflated costs of long-term care services, such as nursing home care or in-home assistance. Research different long-term care insurance options, understand their coverage and benefits, and assess whether it aligns with your needs and budget.

Estate Planning: Estate planning plays a crucial role in managing longevity risk. Establishing a well-structured estate plan can help protect your assets, ensure a smooth transfer of wealth, and potentially minimize tax liabilities. Consult an estate planning attorney to create or update your will, establish trusts, and designate beneficiaries.

Subchapter 34.2: Health Maintenance and Wellness in Retirement

Maintaining good health and wellness in retirement is essential for a fulfilling and enjoyable life. Consider the following:

Healthy Lifestyle Choices: Adopt a healthy lifestyle that includes regular exercise, a balanced diet, sufficient sleep, and stress management techniques. Engage in physical activities you enjoy, such as walking, swimming, or yoga. Consult with healthcare professionals to develop a personalized fitness and nutrition plan.

Preventive Healthcare: Prioritize preventive healthcare measures, including routine check-ups, screenings, and vaccinations. Stay current with recommended health screenings, such as mammograms, colonoscopies, and cholesterol checks. Prevention and early detection can help identify potential health issues and promote well-being.

Mental and Emotional Well-being: Pay attention to your mental and emotional health in retirement. Engage in activities that promote mental stimulation, such as reading, puzzles, or learning new skills. Stay socially connected by maintaining relationships with family and friends, joining community groups, or participating in volunteer work.

Subchapter 34.3: Addressing Potential Healthcare Challenges

As you age, it's essential to be prepared for potential healthcare challenges that may arise. Consider the following:

Healthcare Insurance: Understand your healthcare insurance options, including Medicare and supplemental insurance plans. Educate yourself about Medicare eligibility, enrollment periods, coverage options, and associated costs. Consider working with a Medicare specialist or insurance advisor to ensure you have appropriate coverage that meets your healthcare needs.

Long-Term Care Planning: Address the possibility of needing long-term care services in the future. Research the costs of various long-term care options and consider how you would prefer to receive care, whether at home, in an assisted living facility, or in a nursing home. Explore long-term care insurance, self-funding options, or Medicaid planning strategies to help protect your financial well-being.

Caregiving Considerations: If you anticipate becoming a caregiver for a loved one or needing caregiving support, familiarize yourself with available resources and support networks. Investigate local caregiving services, community programs, and support groups that can provide assistance and guidance.

Remember to prioritize your health and well-being in retirement, as it directly impacts your quality of life. By managing longevity risk through effective financial planning, considering long-term care insurance, and engaging in estate planning, you can mitigate potential challenges associated with living a longer life.

Additionally, focusing on health maintenance and wellness is crucial for a fulfilling retirement. By adopting a healthy lifestyle, engaging in regular physical activity, and prioritizing preventive healthcare measures, you can proactively manage your well-being and reduce the risk of health issues. Please don't neglect your mental and emotional health; they are significant to your wellness.

Preparing for potential healthcare challenges is also essential. Educate yourself about healthcare insurance options, especially Medicare, and consider supplemental insurance plans to ensure comprehensive coverage. Be proactive in long-term care planning, researching costs, and exploring options to address potential future care needs. If you anticipate becoming a caregiver or require caregiving support, familiarize yourself with available resources and support networks.

As you navigate the complexities of longevity and healthcare considerations, seeking guidance from financial advisors, insurance specialists, and healthcare providers is beneficial. They can provide personalized advice based on your circumstances and help you make informed decisions.

By implementing strategies to manage longevity risk, maintaining health and wellness, and addressing potential healthcare challenges, you can enhance your retirement experience and enjoy a fulfilling and secure lifestyle. Remember, taking care of your health and preparing for healthcare-related scenarios are essential to a well-rounded retirement plan.

Here are some websites and valuable resources that provide further assistance and knowledge for longevity and healthcare considerations:

- National Institute on Aging (NIA) - Longevity: The NIA website offers resources and information on aging, longevity, and health. They provide research-based articles, publications, and tools to help individuals understand the aging process and make informed healthcare decisions. (www.nia.nih.gov/health/aging)
- Centers for Disease Control and Prevention (CDC) - Healthy Aging: The CDC provides valuable resources on healthy aging, including information on preventive healthcare, chronic disease management, and lifestyle factors contributing to longevity. Their website offers articles, tips, and tools for promoting healthy aging. (www.cdc.gov/aging)
- World Health Organization (WHO) - Ageing and Health: The WHO offers resources and publications on aging and health, focusing on global perspectives and policies. Their website provides information on healthy aging, healthcare systems, and strategies for addressing the challenges of an aging population. (www.who.int/ageing)
- Mayo Clinic - Healthy Lifestyle: The Mayo Clinic's website offers a wealth of information on healthy living and aging.

They provide articles, expert advice, and practical tips for maintaining physical and mental well-being as you age. (www.mayoclinic.org/healthy-lifestyle)

- National Council on Aging (NCOA) - Aging and Health: The NCOA is a non-profit organization dedicated to improving older adults' health and economic security. Their website offers resources on health and aging, including information on chronic disease management, Medicare, and community-based services. (www.ncoa.org/center-for-healthy-aging)

- Health in Aging Foundation: The Health in Aging Foundation is a non-profit organization that provides information and resources on healthy aging. Their website offers articles, fact sheets, and tools related to healthcare considerations for older adults. (www.healthinaging.org)

- Alzheimer's Association: For information specific to Alzheimer's disease and dementia, the Alzheimer's Association website is a valuable resource. It offers educational materials, caregiver support, research updates, and information on available treatments and services. (www.alz.org)

- Medicare.gov: Medicare is a federal health insurance program for individuals aged sixty-five and older. The Medicare website provides comprehensive information on coverage, enrollment, and healthcare options for older adults. (www.medicare.gov)

- Family Caregiver Alliance: The Family Caregiver Alliance offers resources and support for those caring for aging loved ones. Their website provides information on caregiving, long-term care planning, and resources for managing the healthcare needs of older adults. (www.caregiver.org)

These resources can provide valuable information and guidance on longevity and healthcare considerations. However, consulting with healthcare professionals, including doctors, geriatric specialists, and others, is essential for personalized advice and recommendations based on your specific health needs and circumstances.

Chapter 35: Charitable Contributions in Retirement

Charitable contributions in retirement can be a meaningful way to give back to society and support causes you care about. In this chapter, we will explore the various aspects of making charitable contributions during retirement, including different methods of giving, tax considerations, and real-world scenarios, and provide advice and tips to maximize the impact of your donations.

Subchapter 35.1: Methods of Giving

<u>Cash Donations:</u>

Cash donations are a standard and straightforward method of giving. They involve making monetary contributions directly to charitable organizations. Cash donations are usually tax-deductible, provided the tax authorities recognize the organization as a qualified nonprofit. For example, John, a retiree, donates $5,000 to a local food bank. He receives a tax deduction for this contribution, which reduces his taxable income for the year.

<u>Donor-Advised Funds (DAFs):</u>

A donor-advised fund is a charitable giving vehicle that allows individuals to contribute to a fund and then recommend grants to specific charitable organizations over time. DAFs offer the advantage of centralized giving, as the fund oversees administrative tasks, such as record-keeping and grant distributions.

Example: Sarah, a retiree, establishes a donor-advised fund with a community foundation. She contributes $50,000 to the fund and recommends grants from the fund to support various causes she is enthusiastic about, such as education, healthcare, and the environment.

<u>Charitable Trusts:</u>

Charitable trusts are legal structures that allow individuals to donate assets to a trust, which then distributes income or principal to philanthropic organizations according to the trust's terms. Charitable trusts can provide tax benefits and the ability to support charitable causes while retaining certain income or rights during the donor's lifetime.

Example: David establishes a charitable remainder trust (CRT) with a sizable sum from his retirement savings. The CRT generates annual income for David during his retirement years, and upon his passing, the remaining assets are distributed to charitable organizations of his choice.

Subchapter 35.2: Tax Considerations

Tax Deductions:

Charitable contributions made to qualified nonprofit organizations can often be tax-deductible. The tax benefits vary based on the tax laws of the country or region where you reside. It's essential to consult with a tax advisor or accountant to understand the specific rules and limitations of charitable deductions in your jurisdiction.

Required Minimum Distributions (RMDs):

For retirees who have reached the age of required minimum distributions (RMDs) from retirement accounts such as traditional IRAs or 401(k)s, qualified charitable distributions (QCDs) can be an attractive option. QCDs allow individuals to donate a portion of their RMD directly to a qualified charity, which can help lower taxable income.

Mary, who is 72 years old and has an RMD of $10,000 from her IRA, decides to make a QCD of $5,000 to a charitable organization. By directly transferring the funds, Mary reduces her taxable income by $5,000, potentially resulting in tax savings.

Estate Planning and Legacy Giving:

Charitable contributions can be an integral part of estate planning and legacy giving. By including philanthropic bequests in your will or establishing charitable trusts, you can leave a lasting impact on causes that matter to you while potentially reducing estate taxes.

George, a retiree, includes a provision in his will to donate a sizable portion of his estate to a charitable foundation. This ensures his wealth is used to support philanthropic endeavors after his passing.

Subchapter 35.3: Maximizing the Impact of Charitable Contributions

<u>Research and Due Diligence:</u>

Before making charitable contributions, it's essential to research and carefully evaluate philanthropic organizations to ensure they align with your values and goals. Websites such as Charity Navigator, GuideStar, and the Better Business Bureau's Wise Giving Alliance provide information on nonprofit organizations' transparency, financial health, and impact.

<u>Volunteering and Skills-Based Giving:</u>

In addition to monetary contributions, retirees can consider volunteering their time and expertise to charitable causes. Skills-based giving involves utilizing professional skills and experience to assist nonprofit organizations. This can be rewarding to be effective while leveraging your expertise.

Example: Karen, a retired accountant, volunteers her time to help a local nonprofit with its monetary management. She guides budgeting, financial reporting, and tax compliance, which allows the organization to allocate more resources to its programs and services.

Donor Privacy and Anonymity:

Some individuals prefer to maintain their privacy when making charitable contributions. Many organizations offer the option to donate anonymously, allowing you to support causes without your name being publicly associated with the gift.

Subchapter 35.4: Pros and Cons of Charitable Contributions

<u>Pros:</u>

Fulfilling philanthropic goals and making a positive impact on society.

Tax benefits, including potential deductions for cash contributions and tax savings through qualified charitable distributions.

Legacy building and leaving a lasting impact through planned giving and estate planning.

Opportunities for personal growth, engagement, and connection through volunteering and skills-based giving.

<u>Cons:</u>

Due diligence is necessary to ensure donations are directed to reputable and effective charitable organizations.

The potential for scams or fraudulent charities requires caution and research.

The impact of tax laws and limitations on charitable deductions can vary based on jurisdiction and individual circumstances—potential complexities associated with establishing and managing philanthropic trusts or donor-advised funds.

<u>Here are some websites and valuable resources that provide further assistance and knowledge for charitable contributions in retirement:</u>

- Charity Navigator: Charity Navigator is an independent organization that evaluates and rates charitable organizations based on their financial health, transparency, and impact. Their website offers valuable insights, ratings, and information on various nonprofits to help individuals make informed decisions about their charitable giving.

(www.charitynavigator.org[1])

- GuideStar: GuideStar is a platform that provides comprehensive information on nonprofit organizations. It offers access to nonprofit profiles, financial data, impact reports, and other resources to help donors assess the credibility and effectiveness of charitable organizations. (www.guidestar.org)
- Better Business Bureau's Wise Giving Alliance: The Wise Giving Alliance is a program of the Better Business Bureau that evaluates and accredits charitable organizations based on comprehensive standards for accountability and transparency. Their website provides guidance and resources for making wise giving decisions. (www.give.org)
- Internal Revenue Service (IRS): The IRS website provides information on tax regulations, deductions, and guidelines related to charitable contributions. It offers publications and resources to help retirees understand their donations' tax implications and benefits. (www.irs.gov/charities-non-profits)

- Community Foundations: Community foundations are local organizations that work to improve the quality of life in specific regions. They often provide resources and expertise on charitable giving, donor-advised funds, and philanthropy in retirement. Research community foundations in your area to access local knowledge and support for your generous contributions.
- National Philanthropic Trust: The National Philanthropic Trust is a nonprofit organization that provides philanthropic expertise and support to individuals and organizations. Their website offers resources, research, and guides on charitable

---

1. http://www.charitynavigator.org

giving strategies, including information specific to retirement planning. (www.nptrust.org)

- Estate Planning Attorneys and Financial Advisors: Consulting with professionals such as estate planning attorneys and financial advisors can provide personalized guidance on incorporating charitable contributions into your retirement plans. These professionals can help navigate tax considerations, establish charitable trusts, and ensure your philanthropic goals align with your financial strategy.

Remember to exercise due diligence and research individual charitable organizations before making contributions. The above resources can help guide your decision-making process and provide valuable information. Still, tailoring your giving strategy to your values, financial situation, and desired impact is essential.

<u>Conclusion:</u>

Charitable contributions in retirement allow retirees to give back, support causes they are passionate about, and leave a positive legacy. Retirees can maximize the impact of their contributions and make a meaningful difference in the world by exploring different methods of giving, considering tax implications, conducting thorough research, and actively engaging with charitable organizations. It is advisable to consult with financial and tax professionals to understand the impact and benefits of charitable giving based on individual circumstances.

Chapter 36: Monitoring and Adjusting Your Retirement Plan

Monitoring and adjusting your retirement plan is vital to ensure its effectiveness and alignment with your evolving financial circumstances. This chapter explores the importance of regularly reviewing and updating your retirement plan, adapting to changing economic circumstances, and navigating unexpected events while adjusting course.

Subchapter 36.1: Regularly Reviewing and Updating Your Retirement Plan

Regularly reviewing and updating your retirement plan is essential to keep it on track. Consider the following steps:

Assess Your Goals: Review your retirement goals and aspirations. Have they changed since you initially formulated your plan? Ensure that your plan reflects your current priorities and desired lifestyle.

Evaluate Your Financial Situation: Assess your financial situation periodically. Review your income, expenses, savings, investments, and debts. Determine if any adjustments are necessary to stay on track with your retirement goals.

Review Investment Performance: Monitor the performance of your investment portfolio. Evaluate the returns, diversification, and risk levels of your investments. Consider rebalancing your portfolio to align with your risk tolerance and financial objectives.

Consider Inflation and Cost of Living: Account for inflation and the potential impact on your retirement savings and expenses. Adjust your financial projections and savings goals to maintain purchasing power throughout retirement.

Consult with Professionals: Seek advice from financial advisors, accountants, and other professionals to ensure your retirement plan remains appropriate and effective. They can provide insights, guidance, and expertise tailored to your situation.

Subchapter 36.2: Adapting to Changing Financial Circumstances

Life is dynamic, and your financial circumstances may change over time. Here are some considerations for adapting to changing economic circumstances:

Major Life Events: Significant life events, such as marriage, divorce, the birth of a child, or the loss of a loved one, can impact your financial situation and retirement plan. Evaluate the potential implications of these events and make any necessary adjustments to your project.

Career Changes: Career changes, such as a new job, promotion, or retirement from work, can significantly affect your retirement plan. Assess the financial implications of these changes, such as changes in income, benefits, or retirement account contributions.

Economic Conditions: Economic conditions can fluctuate, impacting investment performance and interest rates. Stay informed about economic trends and their potential impact on your retirement savings. Consider adjusting your investment strategy and financial decisions accordingly.

Subchapter 36.3: Navigating Unexpected Events and Adjusting Course

Life is full of unexpected events, and being prepared to navigate them is essential. Consider the following:

Emergency Funds: Maintain an emergency fund to cover unexpected expenses or financial setbacks. Having readily available cash can provide peace of mind and help weather unexpected challenges without disrupting your retirement plan.

Insurance Coverage: Regularly review your insurance coverage, including health insurance, property insurance, and long-term care insurance. Ensure that your coverage protects you against unforeseen events and liabilities.

Flexibility in Spending: Build flexibility into your retirement budget to accommodate unexpected expenses or changes in financial circumstances. Some wiggle room can help you adjust your spending without derailing your financial plan.

Seek Professional Advice: In the face of unexpected events or significant financial changes, seek guidance from financial advisors, tax professionals, or legal experts. They can provide objective advice and help you navigate through challenging situations.

Remember that retirement planning is ongoing, and adjustments may be necessary. Regularly monitor your retirement plan, adapt to changing financial circumstances, and navigate unexpected events with flexibility and informed decision-making. By staying on top of your retirement plan and making necessary adjustments, you can effectively maintain financial stability and adapt to unforeseen circumstances. Doing so lets you maintain financial security and complete the course corrections required to ensure a successful retirement journey.

Regularly reviewing and updating your retirement plan allows you to assess your goals, evaluate your financial situation, review investment performance, consider inflation and the cost of living, and seek professional advice. These steps ensure your plan remains relevant and aligned with your changing needs and circumstances.

Adapting to changing financial circumstances is crucial. Major life events, such as marriage, divorce, or the birth of a child, can impact your financial situation and require adjustments to your retirement plan. Career changes and economic conditions can also influence your financial outlook. Stay informed, evaluate the potential implications, and make necessary changes to your retirement strategy to maintain stability and meet your goals.

Navigating unexpected events and adjusting courses is a vital aspect of retirement planning. Establishing an emergency fund provides a financial safety net for unforeseen expenses. Reviewing and updating your insurance coverage, including health, property, and long-term care insurance, ensures you're adequately protected. Building flexibility into your retirement budget allows you to accommodate unexpected expenses without derailing your overall plan. Seek guidance from professionals during challenging times to make informed decisions.

<u>Here are some websites and valuable resources that provide further assistance and knowledge for monitoring and adjusting your retirement plan:</u>

- Financial Industry Regulatory Authority (FINRA): FINRA offers a variety of resources and tools to help individuals monitor and adjust their retirement plans. Their website provides educational materials, retirement calculators, and tips for managing investments and adjusting your plan as needed. (www.finra.org)
- Employee Benefit Research Institute (EBRI): The EBRI website offers research, publications, and retirement planning and monitoring tools. They provide insights into retirement trends, savings strategies, and ways to assess and adjust your plan based on changing circumstances. (www.ebri.org)
- Social Security Administration (SSA): The SSA website is valuable for understanding and monitoring your Social Security benefits. It provides information on eligibility, benefit calculations, retirement age considerations, and how to create a mySocialSecurity account to access your personalized benefits statement. (www.ssa.gov)
- U.S. Department of Labor - Employee Benefits Security Administration (EBSA): The EBSA offers resources and information on retirement plans, including guidance on

monitoring and managing employer-sponsored retirement accounts such as 401(k)s. Their website provides educational materials, FAQs, and tools to help individuals understand and evaluate their retirement benefits. (www.dol.gov/agencies/ebsa)

- AARP: AARP is a nonprofit organization supporting fifty and older individuals. Their website offers a wide range of resources and tools for retirement planning, including articles, retirement calculators, and tips for monitoring and adjusting your plan as you navigate different life stages. (www.aarp.org/retirement)

- Financial Planning Association (FPA): The FPA is a professional organization for financial planners. Their website provides resources for finding a qualified financial planner who can assist you in monitoring and adjusting your retirement plan. They also offer articles, guides, and educational materials on retirement planning and investment management. (www.financialplanningassociation.org)

- Vanguard: Vanguard is an investment management company that offers a variety of resources and tools for retirement planning. Their website provides retirement calculators, educational materials, and insights on managing and adjusting your investment portfolio as you approach and enter retirement. (www.vanguard.com/retirement)

- Charles Schwab: Charles Schwab is another reputable investment management firm that provides retirement planning and monitoring resources. Their website offers retirement calculators, articles, and insights on adjusting your investment strategy based on your retirement goals and changing market conditions. (www.schwab.com/retirement-planning)

It's important to note that while these resources can provide valuable guidance and information, consulting with a qualified financial advisor or planner is recommended to receive personalized advice tailored to your specific financial situation, goals, and risk tolerance.

Chapter 37: Managing Divorce In Retirement

Divorce can significantly impact one's financial situation, especially during retirement. This chapter aims to provide a comprehensive understanding of managing divorce in retirement. It will explore various aspects such as dividing assets, retirement accounts, alimony, real-world scenarios, advice, tips, tricks, and the pros and cons of navigating divorce in retirement.

Subchapter 37.1: Dividing Retirement Assets

<u>Understanding Marital Property:</u>

In divorce, marital property refers to assets acquired during the marriage. It includes retirement accounts, pensions, investment portfolios, real estate, and other valuable assets. Understanding the laws and regulations regarding marital property division is crucial to ensure a fair distribution of assets.

Real-World Scenario: Sarah and John are divorcing after 30 years of marriage. They have accumulated substantial retirement assets, including 401(k) accounts, pensions, and investments. They consult with financial advisors and attorneys to determine how to divide these assets equitably based on their state's laws and individual financial needs.

<u>Tips and Advice:</u>

Gather all relevant financial documents, including retirement account statements, investment portfolios, and property deeds.

Consult a qualified divorce attorney specializing in financial matters to guide you through the asset division process.

Consider engaging the services of a financial planner to help you understand the long-term financial implications of various asset division scenarios.

1.2 QDROs and Retirement Account Division:

Qualified Domestic Relations Orders (QDROs) are legal documents that allow the division of retirement accounts, such as 401(k)s and pensions, in a divorce. QDROs specify how the funds will be allocated between the divorcing parties.

Real-World Scenario: Mark and Lisa are going through a divorce. Mark has a 401(k) account with a significant balance. Their divorce settlement specifies that a portion of Mark's 401(k) will be transferred to Lisa's retirement account (IRA) through a QDRO.

Tips and Advice:

Seek guidance from a qualified attorney experienced in QDROs to ensure compliance with the specific rules and regulations governing the retirement account division.

Understand the tax implications of transferring retirement funds and consult a tax professional to minimize potential tax consequences.

Subchapter 37.2: Alimony and Spousal Support

Alimony in Retirement:

Alimony, also known as spousal support or maintenance, is a payment made by one spouse to the other after divorce. It is intended to provide financial support to the lower-earning spouse. Alimony can have significant implications for retirement planning.

Real-World Scenario: Susan and Michael are divorcing, and Susan has been a stay-at-home parent for many years. As part of the divorce settlement, Michael agrees to pay alimony to Susan, ensuring she has a stable income during retirement.

Tips and Advice:

Understand the laws and guidelines related to alimony in your jurisdiction, as they vary from state to state.

Consider the financial implications of alimony on your retirement savings and income. Work with a financial planner to evaluate the long-term effects of alimony payments on your retirement goals.

<u>Social Security Benefits and Divorce:</u>

Divorced individuals may be eligible for Social Security benefits based on their ex-spouse's earnings record. Understanding the eligibility requirements and potential benefits is crucial for maximizing retirement income.

Real-World Scenario: James and Emily divorced after 20 years of marriage. Emily has not worked consistently and has a lower Social Security earnings history. As a divorced spouse, Emily can receive Social Security benefits based on James' earnings record, potentially increasing her retirement income.

Tips and Advice:

Review the eligibility criteria for Social Security benefits based on an ex-spouse's earnings record. Generally, you must have been married for at least ten years and not currently remarried to qualify.

Calculate the benefits of claiming Social Security based on your record versus the ex-spouses. Consult a Social Security specialist to understand the best strategy for maximizing your benefits.

Subchapter 37.3: Pros and Cons of Divorce in Retirement

<u>Pros:</u>

Increased financial independence: Divorce may allow individuals to have greater control over their finances and make independent decisions about their retirement planning.

Fresh start: Divorce can be a chance to reassess financial goals, restructure investments, and create a new retirement plan that aligns with personal aspirations.

<u>Cons:</u>

Asset division: Divorce often involves dividing assets, including retirement accounts, which can reduce overall retirement savings and impact long-term financial security.

Lower income: Alimony or spousal support payments may reduce the income available for retirement savings and increase financial strain during retirement.

Conclusion:

Managing divorce in retirement requires careful consideration of various financial aspects, including dividing assets, understanding alimony and spousal support, and exploring options such as Social Security benefits. It is essential to consult with professionals, including attorneys, financial advisors, and tax specialists, to navigate the complexities of divorce and ensure a fair and secure financial future in retirement. Taking proactive steps, understanding the potential pros and cons, and seeking expert guidance can help individuals effectively manage divorce and maintain financial stability during retirement.

Here are some websites and valuable resources that can provide further assistance and knowledge on managing divorce in retirement:

- American Bar Association (ABA) - Section of Family Law: The ABA's Section offers a wealth of resources on divorce and related financial matters. Their website provides articles, publications, and information on finding a divorce attorney. Visit: https://www.americanbar.org/groups/family_law/
- National Association of Divorce Professionals (NADP): NADP is an organization that brings together professionals specializing in divorce-related fields, including attorneys, financial advisors, and mediators. Their website offers resources and a directory to find professionals experienced in managing divorce in retirement. Visit: https://thenadp.com/
- DivorceMag: DivorceMag provides articles, guides, and resources covering various aspects of divorce, including finances and retirement. Their website offers a comprehensive collection of information to help individuals navigate divorce in retirement. Visit: https://www.divorcemag.com/

- Financial Planning Association (FPA): The FPA is an organization of financial planning professionals. Their website provides resources and tools to help individuals understand and navigate the financial aspects of divorce, including retirement planning. Visit: https://www.financialplanningassociation.org/
- National Endowment for Financial Education (NEFE): NEFE offers resources and educational materials on various financial topics, including divorce and retirement planning. Their website provides articles, publications, and tools to help individuals make informed financial decisions during and after divorce. Visit: https://www.nefe.org/
- Pension Rights Center: The Pension Rights Center is a nonprofit organization that protects and advocates pension rights. Their website provides information and resources related to pensions and retirement benefits, which can be helpful when managing divorce in retirement. Visit: https://www.pensionrights.org/

It's important to note that while these resources can provide valuable information, consulting with qualified professionals such as attorneys, financial advisors, and tax specialists is crucial for personalized advice tailored to your situation.

Chapter 38: Retirement Abroad

Retiring abroad can be an exciting and life-changing decision. This chapter aims to provide a comprehensive understanding of retirement abroad, exploring various aspects such as choosing a retirement destination, financial considerations, healthcare, real-world scenarios, advice, tips, tricks, and the pros and cons associated with retiring in a foreign country.

Subchapter 38.1: Choosing a Retirement Destination

<u>Researching Potential Countries:</u>

When considering retiring abroad, it's essential to research and explores potential countries that align with your lifestyle preferences, budget, and healthcare needs. Factors to consider include the cost of living, climate, culture, safety, healthcare infrastructure, and ease of integration for expatriates.

Real-World Scenario: John and Mary dream of retiring to a tropical destination with a lower cost of living. They research countries such as Costa Rica, Panama, and Thailand, considering factors like healthcare quality, affordability, climate, and recreational opportunities.

Tips and Advice:

Utilize online resources, guidebooks, and expatriate forums to gather information about potential retirement destinations.

Consider visiting prospective countries as a tourist before making a final decision. This allows you to experience the culture, infrastructure, and lifestyle firsthand.

<u>Financial Considerations:</u>

Assessing the financial implications of retiring abroad is crucial. Factors to consider include exchange rates, tax implications, cost of living, and access to banking and financial services in the chosen country.

Real-World Scenario: Sarah plans to retire in Portugal. She consults with a financial advisor to understand the tax implications, potential currency fluctuations, and the best strategies to manage her retirement savings in a foreign country.

Tips and Advice:

Consult with a financial advisor specializing in international finance to understand the tax implications of retiring abroad and how to structure your finances accordingly.

Research the cost of living in your chosen destination and develop a realistic budget that aligns with your retirement income and goals.

Subchapter 38.2: Healthcare Considerations

<u>Access to Healthcare:</u>

Healthcare availability and quality vary from country to country. Understanding the healthcare system, insurance options, and access to medical facilities and services is crucial for a successful retirement abroad.

Real-World Scenario: James and Linda choose to retire in Mexico. They research the local healthcare system, obtain comprehensive health insurance covering medical expenses in their new country, and identify reputable hospitals and doctors.

Tips and Advice:

Research the healthcare system of your chosen country, including the availability of doctors, hospitals, and specialized medical services.

Consider obtaining international health insurance to ensure comprehensive coverage and access to medical facilities in your chosen country and during travel.

<u>Language and Cultural Considerations:</u>

Language and cultural differences can impact your experience as a retiree abroad. Consider the language in your retirement destination and assess your comfort level with learning and integrating into a new culture.

Real-World Scenario: Mark and Emma choose to retire in France. They enroll in language classes to learn French, which enhances their ability to navigate daily life, communicate with locals, and access healthcare services.

Tips and Advice:

Take language classes or use language-learning apps to familiarize yourself with the local language. This will enhance your ability to interact with locals, access services, and integrate into the community.

Embrace the local culture and customs, which can enrich your retirement experience and facilitate meaningful connections with the local community.

Subchapter 38.3: Pros and Cons of Retirement Abroad

<u>Pros:</u>

Lower cost of living: Many countries offer a lower living cost than the United States or other developed nations, allowing retirees to stretch their retirement savings further.

New experiences and cultural enrichment: Retiring abroad offers the opportunity to immerse yourself in a new culture, explore new traditions, and experience a unique way of life.

Potential healthcare savings: Some countries provide quality healthcare services at a lower cost than in your home country, allowing you to access necessary medical care at a more affordable price.

Adventure and travel opportunities: Retirement abroad opens up opportunities for travel and exploration, as you are already in a different region or continent.

<u>Cons:</u>

Language and cultural barriers: Adjusting to a new language and cultural norms can be challenging, mainly if you are not accustomed to living in a foreign country.

Distance from family and friends: Retiring abroad may mean being far away from loved ones, impacting social support and connections.

Potential legal and bureaucratic challenges: Navigating legal processes, visa requirements, and bureaucratic systems in a foreign country can be complex and time-consuming.

Healthcare considerations: While some countries offer excellent healthcare, others may need more resources or different standards of care, requiring thorough research and planning.

Conclusion:

Retiring abroad can be a fulfilling and enriching experience, providing opportunities for new adventures, cultural immersion, and potentially lower living costs. However, it requires careful planning, research, and consideration of several factors such as healthcare, financial implications, language, and cultural differences. By thoroughly assessing the pros and cons, seeking professional guidance, and embracing the opportunities that retirement abroad offers, individuals can embark on a rewarding chapter of their lives in a foreign country.

<u>Here are some websites and valuable resources that can provide further assistance and knowledge on retiring abroad:</u>

- International Living: International Living is a trusted resource for individuals considering retirement abroad. Their website offers articles, guides, and resources on various retirement destinations, including information on the cost of living, healthcare, and ex-pat communities. Visit: https://internationalliving.com/
- Retire Overseas: Retire Overseas provides comprehensive information and resources for retirees looking to live abroad. Their website offers destination guides, articles, and a community forum to connect with other retirees and ex-pats. Visit: https://www.retireoverseas.com/
- U.S. Department of State - Bureau of Consular Affairs: The U.S. Department of State's website provides valuable travel information, living abroad and retiring overseas. It offers country-specific resources, including information on visa requirements and safety considerations. Visit:

https://travel.state.gov/content/travel/en/international-travel/while-abroad/retirement-abroad.html

- Expat Exchange: Expat Exchange is an online community and resource for expatriates. Their website provides forums, destination guides, and articles on retirement abroad, including real-life experiences and advice from other ex-pats. Visit: https://www.expatexchange.com/

- Medicare.gov: If you are a U.S. citizen and eligible for Medicare, the official Medicare website provides information on how Medicare coverage works outside the United States. It outlines the rules and options for healthcare coverage while living abroad. Visit: https://www.medicare.gov/coverage/travel-when-you-need-care-outside-the-us

- InternationalLiving.com's Best Places to Retire Abroad: InternationalLiving.com publishes an annual list of the best places to retire abroad. It provides insights into various countries and destinations based on the cost of living, healthcare quality, climate, and lifestyle. Visit: https://internationalliving.com/the-worlds-best-places-to-retire/

Remember to consult with financial advisors, tax specialists, and legal experts who specialize in international retirement to ensure you have personalized advice tailored to your situation and retirement goals.

Chapter 39: Embracing Cultural and Artistic Experiences in Retirement

Retirement offers a unique opportunity to explore and embrace cultural and artistic experiences. This chapter aims to comprehensively understand how retirees can enrich their lives through various art forms, including visual arts, performing arts, literature, and more. It will explore the benefits, real-world scenarios, advice, tips, tricks, and the pros and cons of embracing cultural and artistic experiences in retirement.

Subchapter 39.1: Exploring Visual Arts

<u>Visiting Art Museums and Galleries:</u>

Retirees can visit art museums and galleries to explore different artistic movements, discover renowned works of art, and gain inspiration from various artists. Many cities and towns offer local art exhibits, making it accessible and convenient for retirees to engage in visual arts.

Real-World Scenario: Linda, a retiree, develops a passion for painting. She visits local art museums and galleries, attends art exhibitions, and participates in workshops to learn different painting techniques.

Tips and Advice:

Research local art museums, galleries, and cultural centers in your area to discover upcoming exhibits and events.

Consider joining art institutions to enjoy unique benefits such as discounted admission, exclusive previews, and access to educational programs.

<u>Creating Art: Painting, Sculpting, and More:</u>

Retirement is an ideal time to explore one's artistic side. Engaging in painting, sculpting, pottery, or photography can be a creative outlet and a means of personal expression and self-discovery.

Real-World Scenario: John, upon retiring, takes up photography as a hobby. He explores different techniques, captures beautiful images, and shares them with friends and family.

Tips and Advice:

Start with beginner-friendly art forms or take classes to learn new techniques and develop your skills.

Join local art groups or workshops to connect with other artists, share experiences, and receive constructive feedback.

Subchapter 39.2: Appreciating Performing Arts

Attending Theater and Performing Arts Shows:

Retirees can embrace the performing arts by attending theater shows, ballet performances, opera, concerts, and other live performances. It offers a chance to immerse oneself in storytelling, music, and the talent of performers.

Real-World Scenario: Sarah and David, retired music enthusiasts, regularly attend classical concerts and opera performances. They enjoy the live performances and the cultural experiences they offer.

Tips and Advice:

Check local event listings, community theaters, and performing arts centers for upcoming shows and performances.

Consider subscribing to season tickets or becoming a local theater or performing arts organization member for discounted tickets and priority seating.

Participating in Performing Arts:

Retirement can also be an opportunity to explore one's talents and participate in performing arts activities. Joining community theater groups, choirs, or dance classes allows retirees to engage in artistic expression and foster a sense of community.

Real-World Scenario: Peter, after retiring, joins a local community theater group and participates in various stage productions. He enjoys the camaraderie with fellow performers and the thrill of being on stage.

Tips and Advice:

Research local community theater groups, choir ensembles, or dance studios that offer classes or opportunities for adult learners.

Embrace the learning process, and don't hesitate to step outside your comfort zone. The focus is on personal growth and enjoyment.

Subchapter 39.3: Literary Pursuits

<u>Reading and Book Clubs:</u>

Retirement provides more time for reading and literary exploration. Joining book clubs or starting with like-minded individuals can be rewarding for discovering new authors, discussing literature, and fostering intellectual stimulation.

Real-World Scenario: an avid reader, Jane joins a book club in her retirement community. They meet regularly to discuss various literary works, broadening their reading horizons.

Tips and Advice:

Look for local book clubs at libraries, community centers, or retirement communities. Online book clubs are also an option for connecting with fellow readers.

Experiment with different genres and authors to expand your reading repertoire.

<u>Writing and Creative Writing Groups:</u>

Retirement offers an ideal time to explore writing as a form of self-expression. Engaging in creative writing or memoir writing can be personally fulfilling and provide an avenue for sharing one's stories and experiences.

Real-World Scenario: Robert, upon retiring, takes up authoring short stories. He joins a local creative writing group, where he receives feedback and encouragement from fellow writers.

Tips and Advice:

Explore different writing genres such as fiction, poetry, or personal essays to find what resonates with you. Consider joining a writing group or workshop to receive constructive feedback and connect with other writers.

Subchapter 39.4: Pros and Cons of Embracing Cultural and Artistic Experiences

<u>Pros:</u>

Personal enrichment: Engaging in cultural and artistic experiences can bring joy, personal fulfillment, and a sense of purpose in retirement.

Intellectual stimulation: Exploring different art forms and engaging with creativity can provide ongoing intellectual stimulation and cognitive benefits.

Social connections: Participating in art-related activities offers opportunities to connect with like-minded individuals, fostering new friendships and a sense of community.

Personal growth: Embracing cultural and artistic experiences allows retirees to explore new interests, develop skills, and continue learning.

<u>Cons:</u>

Financial considerations: Some art-related activities, such as attending performances or purchasing art supplies, may come with associated costs that must be considered within a retirement budget.

Time commitment: Engaging in artistic pursuits and attending cultural events may require a considerable time commitment, which retirees should balance with other aspects of their retirement lifestyle.

Accessibility: Access to cultural and artistic experiences may vary depending on location and available resources, especially in rural or remote areas.

Conclusion:

Embracing cultural and artistic experiences in retirement can bring many benefits, including personal enrichment, intellectual stimulation, social connections, and personal growth. Retirees can discover new passions, express their creativity, and find fulfillment in retirement by exploring visual arts, participating in performing arts, and pursuing literary pursuits. It is crucial to consider the pros and cons, plan for associated costs, and seek out local resources and communities that support these endeavors. Ultimately, the journey of embracing cultural and artistic experiences can lead to a more vibrant and fulfilling retirement.

Here are some websites and valuable resources that can provide further assistance and knowledge on embracing cultural and artistic experiences in retirement:

- AARP: AARP offers a range of resources and articles on arts and culture for retirees, including information on museums, performing arts, literary activities, and more. Visit: https://www.aarp.org/
- Local Arts Councils and Cultural Organizations: Check your local arts and cultural organizations' websites for information on upcoming events, art classes, workshops, and community programs. These organizations often provide resources and support for individuals interested in engaging with the arts.
- Meetup: Meetup is a platform that connects people with similar interests, including various arts-related activities. You can search for local meetup groups focused on art, literature, theater, or any specific artistic interest you have. Visit: https://www.meetup.com/
- The National Endowment for the Arts (NEA): The NEA is an independent agency of the U.S. federal government that supports and promotes artistic excellence, creativity, and cultural preservation. Their website offers resources, grant

information, and publications related to the arts. Visit: https://www.arts.gov/

- Creative Aging Organizations: Creative aging organizations, such as the National Center for Creative Aging (NCCA) or local affiliates, focus on promoting arts and creativity for older adults. They provide resources, workshops, and programs encouraging artistic engagement in retirement. Visit: https://www.creativeaging.org/

- Local Libraries: Libraries often host events, book clubs, and workshops related to literature, writing, and other artistic pursuits. Check your local library's website or inquire with librarians about their offerings.

- Online Learning Platforms: Coursera, Udemy, and Skillshare offer online courses on various artistic subjects, including painting, photography, writing, and more. These platforms allow you to learn at your own pace and explore new artistic interests from the comfort of your home.

- Artist Communities and Retreats: Explore artist communities and retreats that offer specialized programs for retirees interested in pursuing their artistic passions. These communities provide an immersive environment for creative exploration and often offer workshops, mentorship, and access to resources.

Remember to explore local resources such as community centers, art schools, retirement communities, and local newspapers or magazines that may provide information on cultural events and opportunities in your area. Engaging with local artists, attending art fairs or festivals, and connecting with local art galleries can also expand your cultural and artistic experiences in retirement.

Chapter 40: Technology and Social Media for Seniors

This chapter aims to explore the role of technology and social media in the lives of seniors. It will provide a detailed overview of various technologies, their benefits, and how seniors can navigate the digital world. This chapter will also address real-world scenarios, provide advice, tips, and tricks, and discuss the pros and cons of technology and social media for seniors.

Subchapter 40.1: The Benefits of Technology for Seniors

<u>Communication and Connectivity:</u>

Technology connects seniors with family, friends, and the broader community. With tools such as video calls, emails, and social media platforms, seniors can bridge geographical distances, share experiences, and maintain meaningful relationships.

Real-World Scenario: Mary, a retired grandmother, uses video calls to connect with her grandchildren who live in a different state. She gets to see their faces, hear their voices, and participate in their lives, even from afar.

Advice and Tips:

Choose user-friendly devices and platforms that suit your needs and preferences.

Take advantage of tutorials and online resources to use different communication tools effectively.

<u>Access to Information and Learning:</u>

Technology provides seniors with access to a wealth of information and learning opportunities. Online resources, educational platforms, and digital libraries offer a wide range of content, allowing seniors to pursue their interests, learn new skills, and stay intellectually engaged.

Real-World Scenario: John, a retired engineer, uses online learning platforms to take history and computer programming courses. He enjoys the flexibility of learning at his own pace and expanding his knowledge.

Advice and Tips:

Explore online learning platforms like Coursera, Udemy, or Khan Academy for courses that align with your interests.

Use search engines to find information on specific topics or join online forums and communities to discuss with like-minded individuals.

Subchapter 40.2: Navigating Social Media Platforms

<u>Connecting with Peers:</u>

Social media platforms allow seniors to connect with peers with similar interests, hobbies, or life experiences. Online groups and communities focused on topics like travel, gardening, or book clubs allow seniors to find like-minded individuals and engage in discussions.

Real-World Scenario: a retired teacher, Sarah, joins a Facebook group for past educators. She connects with former colleagues, shares teaching resources, and participates in discussions about education-related topics.

Advice and Tips:

Choose social media platforms that are popular among your age group or focus on specific interests.

Be mindful of online privacy and security. Adjust privacy settings to control the visibility of your personal information.

<u>Sharing Life Experiences:</u>

Seniors can use social media to share their life experiences, stories, and wisdom with a broader audience. Blogging platforms like

WordPress or Blogger allow seniors to create personal blogs and share their thoughts on several topics.

Real-World Scenario: David, a retired journalist, starts a blog about his travel adventures, providing tips and recommendations for fellow seniors who enjoy exploring the world.

Advice and Tips:

Consider starting a blog or writing guest posts for existing blogs to share your experiences and insights.

Engage with your readers by responding to comments and fostering discussions around your blog posts.

Subchapter 3: Pros and Cons of Technology and Social Media for Seniors

Subchapter 40.3: Pros and Cons of Technology and Social Media for Seniors

Pros:

Improved communication and connectivity with family and friends, regardless of geographical distances.

Access to a vast amount of information and learning opportunities, promoting intellectual stimulation and personal growth.

Opportunities to connect with like-minded individuals, fostering new friendships and a sense of community.

Enhanced ability to share experiences, stories, and wisdom with a broader audience.

Cons:

Potential for technology-related frustrations and learning curves, especially for seniors less familiar with digital devices and platforms.

Privacy and security concerns, as personal information can be vulnerable online. Seniors need to be cautious and aware of potential risks.

Potential for social isolation if the technology becomes a substitute for in-person interactions. Seniors should find a balance between online and offline social connections.

Conclusion:

This chapter highlights the benefits of technology and social media for seniors. It explores how technology enables communication, connectivity, access to information, and learning opportunities. Navigating social media platforms can help seniors connect with peers, share life experiences, and engage in online communities. However, being mindful of technology's potential challenges and risks is essential. Seniors should use user-friendly devices, seek support and guidance, and prioritize privacy and security. By embracing technology and social media, seniors can enhance their lives, stay connected, and actively participate in the digital world.

<u>Here are some websites and valuable resources that can provide further assistance and knowledge on technology and social media for seniors:</u>

- AARP Technology Resources: AARP offers a range of technology resources tailored for seniors, including articles, tutorials, and guides on using devices, social media, online safety, and more. Visit: https://www.aarp.org/home-family/personal-technology/
- SeniorNet: SeniorNet is a nonprofit organization providing seniors with technology education. They offer computer classes, workshops, and online resources to help seniors learn and navigate the digital world. Visit: https://seniornet.org/
- TechBoomers: TechBoomers provides free tutorials and courses on various technology topics, including social media platforms like Facebook, Twitter, and Instagram. The tutorials are designed specifically for beginners and seniors. Visit: https://techboomers.com/

- GetConnected: GetConnected is a website and TV show that provides technology advice and tutorials for all ages, including seniors. Their website features articles and videos covering a wide range of tech-related topics. Visit: https://getconnectedmedia.com/

- Older Adults Technology Services (OATS): OATS is a nonprofit organization offering seniors technology training programs. They provide classes, workshops, and resources to help seniors build digital skills and confidence. Visit: https://oats.org/

- Senior Planet: Senior Planet is an online community and resource center for older adults interested in technology and digital literacy. They offer articles, tutorials, and webinars on various technology topics, including social media. Visit: https://seniorplanet.org/

- YouTube: YouTube is a valuable resource for finding video tutorials and guides on using technology and social media platforms. Many content creators focus on teaching seniors how to navigate devices, apps, and social media effectively.

- Local Senior Centers and Community Centers: Check with your local senior centers and community centers for technology classes, workshops, or one-on-one training sessions tailored to seniors. These centers often have resources and knowledgeable staff who can assist with technology-related questions.

Remember to approach technology and social media with an open mind and a willingness to learn. Take your time, start with basic skills, and gradually explore more advanced features. Don't hesitate to reach out for assistance or join online communities where you can connect with other seniors who are also learning and embracing technology.

Chapter 41: Exploring and Preserving Family History

This chapter delves into the importance of exploring and preserving family history. It highlights the value of understanding one's roots, documenting personal stories, and passing down the legacy to future generations. This chapter will provide detailed information and tips on exploring and preserving family history, including real-world scenarios, advice, and pros and cons.

Subchapter 41.1: The Significance of Family History

Understanding Identity and Heritage:

Exploring family history helps individuals better understand their identity and heritage. Learning about ancestors' struggles, achievements, and cultural traditions provides a sense of connection and belonging.

Real-World Scenario: Sarah, a retiree, embarks on a journey to trace her family's history. Through her research, she discovers that her great-grandfather was an immigrant who overcame numerous obstacles to build a successful business. This knowledge strengthens her pride in her family's heritage and inspires her resilience journey.

Advice and Tips:

Begin by interviewing older family members to gather their memories and stories.

Use online genealogy resources like Ancestry.com or FamilySearch.org to build your family tree and access historical records.

Preserving Memories and Stories:

Family history preservation ensures that personal stories and memories are passed down through generations. By documenting family narratives, individuals can preserve their unique experiences and keep them alive for future family members.

Real-World Scenario: Mark, a retiree, starts a family history blog sharing stories, photos, and videos from his ancestors. He encourages family members to contribute their memories, creating a collaborative platform to preserve their collective heritage.

Advice and Tips:

Create a family archive by organizing and digitizing old photographs, letters, and documents.

Consider using video or audio recording tools to capture interviews with family members, allowing them to share their stories in their voices.

Subchapter 41.2: Techniques for Exploring Family History

Conducting Research:

Research is a fundamental aspect of exploring family history. By delving into historical records, census data, immigration records, and local archives, individuals can uncover valuable information about their ancestors' lives.

Real-World Scenario: Emily, a retiree passionate about history, visits local libraries, archives, and genealogy centers to access primary sources and search for records related to her family. She also collaborates with other genealogists online, sharing information and insights.

Advice and Tips:

Utilize online genealogy databases and websites to access historical records and connect with other researchers.

Visit local libraries, historical societies, and archives to access resources specific to your family's region.

DNA Testing and Genetic Genealogy:

DNA testing has become increasingly popular as a tool for exploring family history. Genetic genealogy can provide insights into ethnic origins, connect individuals with distant relatives, and help expand family trees.

Real-World Scenario: James, a retiree, takes a DNA test and discovers new cousins living in another country. He gains valuable information about his family's migration history and builds new relationships by connecting with them.

Advice and Tips:

Choose a reputable DNA testing company and review their privacy policies before submitting a sample.

Be prepared for unexpected results or potential discoveries that may affect your perception of family relationships.

Subchapter 41.3: Preserving Family History

<u>Documenting Oral Histories:</u>

Oral histories are a powerful way to preserve family memories and personal stories. Recording interviews with older family members allow their unique perspectives to be captured and shared with future generations.

Real-World Scenario: Lisa, a retiree, interviews her grandparents and other elderly relatives, capturing their childhood memories, life experiences, and cultural traditions. She transcribes the interviews and creates a family history book for her extended family.

Advice and Tips:

Prepare a list of questions to guide the interview process and encourage storytelling.

Consider using smartphone apps or voice recorders to capture high-quality audio recordings.

<u>Creating Digital Archives:</u>

Digital archiving provides a convenient and accessible way to preserve family history materials. Individuals can create a digital archive that can be easily shared and maintained by digitizing documents, photographs, and recordings.

Real-World Scenario: John, a retiree, digitizes his family's album of photographs and organizes them into albums on his computer. He shares these albums with his children and grandchildren, ensuring the family memories are readily accessible to future generations.

Advice and Tips:

Invest in quality scanners or scanning services to digitize photographs and documents.

Organize digital files into folders with clear labeling and use backup systems to protect against data loss.

Pros and Cons of Exploring and Preserving Family History:

<u>Pros:</u>

Deepens understanding of personal identity and heritage.

Preserves family stories and memories for future generations.

Enhances connections among family members by sharing a common history.

Provides opportunities for self-discovery and personal growth.

<u>Cons:</u>

Research can be time-consuming and require significant effort.

Some historical records may be challenging to access or may not exist.

Genetic genealogy results may reveal unexpected family secrets or challenge existing family narratives.

Conclusion:

Preserving family history emphasizes the significance of exploring and preserving family history. It highlights the role of family history in understanding identity, maintaining memories, and connecting generations. By utilizing research techniques, conducting interviews, and embracing digital preservation methods, individuals can embark on a rewarding journey of discovery and create a lasting legacy for their families. Remember to cherish the stories and experiences shared by older family members and encourage younger generations to continue the tradition of exploring and preserving their family history.

Here are some resources and websites that can assist you in researching and exploring your family history:

- Ancestry.com (www.ancestry.com): Ancestry is one of the most popular genealogy websites, providing access to a vast collection of historical records, family trees, and DNA testing services.

- FamilySearch.org (www.familysearch.org): FamilySearch, operated by The Church of Jesus Christ of Latter-day Saints, offers a comprehensive collection of genealogical records from around the world, including census data, birth and death records, and more. It is a free resource for genealogical research.

- MyHeritage.com (www.myheritage.com): MyHeritage offers access to an extensive historical records database, family trees, and DNA testing services. It also provides tools for creating and sharing family history.

- National Archives (www.archives.gov): The National Archives is the official repository of the United States government's records. It provides access to a wide range of historical documents, including census records, military records, immigration records, and more.

- Library of Congress (www.loc.gov): The Library of Congress is the largest in the United States and houses a vast collection of historical resources, including books, manuscripts, maps, newspapers, and photographs.

- Cyndi's List (www.cyndislist.com): Cyndi's List is a comprehensive directory of online resources for genealogical research. It categorizes and links thousands of websites related to family history and genealogy.

- Findmypast (www.findmypast.com): Findmypast offers a broad collection of historical records, including birth, marriage, death, military, and newspapers from various countries.
- Archives.com (www.archives.com): Archives.com provides access to a wide range of historical records, including vital records, census data, military records, and more. It offers both free and subscription-based services.
- Fold3 (www.fold3.com): Fold3 specializes in military records and provides access to many military-related documents, including service records, pension files, and historical newspapers.
- GenealogyBank (www.genealogybank.com): GenealogyBank focuses on historical newspapers and provides access to an extensive collection of digitized newspapers from various regions and periods.

Acknowledgments:

I thank everyone who supported me in authoring this book. I want to thank my wonderful wife, who has been my constant companion and cheerleader throughout this journey. She has given me her love, encouragement, and constructive feedback and has always believed in me and my vision. Without her, this book would not have been possible.

I also want to acknowledge the invaluable resources and guidance I have received from various experts and organizations in retirement planning. They have generously shared their insights, experiences, and best practices with me and helped me shape this book's content and structure. I am incredibly grateful to all of them.

Additionally, I want to thank my friends and family for their support and encouragement. They were there for me during this project's highs and lows and offered me advice, help, and humor. They have also been my first readers and critics and have given me honest and constructive feedback. I am lucky to have such an excellent network of people who care about me and my work.

Finally, thank you, the reader, for choosing this book and allowing me to share my knowledge and passion. This book is valuable, and enjoyable and will help you achieve your retirement goals and dreams. Thank you for your trust and attention.

Epilogue:

<u>Embracing the Journey of Retirement</u>

As we reach the end of this handbook, reflecting on your remarkable journey is essential. Armed with knowledge and wisdom, you've navigated the vast landscape of retirement planning to make informed decisions about your future. You've explored the facets of this new chapter in your life, from financial strategies to health and wellness, social connections, and personal growth.

Now that you've absorbed the wealth of information within these pages, it's time to embrace the realities and joys of retirement. Remember, retirement is not merely a destination but a dynamic and evolving journey. It's a time for self-discovery, pursuing passions, cherishing relationships, and positively impacting the world around you.

While this handbook provides a comprehensive guide, it's essential to remember that your retirement journey is uniquely yours. Each retiree experiences joys, challenges, and triumphs. Use this handbook as a foundation but feel empowered to adapt and customize the information to align with your specific needs, dreams, and aspirations.

Retirement offers an opportunity to redefine yourself, explore new horizons, and nurture your well-being. It's a time to prioritize what truly matters, spending quality time with loved ones, engaging in meaningful activities, or contributing to causes close to your heart.

As you embark on this next phase, remember the importance of balance. Embrace leisure and relaxation, but also challenge yourself to learn and grow. Seek new experiences, indulge in hobbies, and find ways to give back to your community. Remember that retirement is not the end of productivity but an invitation to pursue passions and make a difference in the lives of others.

Throughout your retirement, continue to review and update your plan. Circumstances change, and it's essential to remain flexible and adapt accordingly. Regularly reassess your financial goals, evaluate your healthcare needs, and nurture your emotional well-being.

Approach retirement with a positive mindset and an open heart. Embrace the freedom to explore, dream, and savor simple pleasures. Surround yourself with a supportive network of friends and loved ones who uplift and inspire you.

Congratulations on completing this handbook and embarking on this exciting chapter of your life. Remember, retirement is a journey to be embraced, cherished, and celebrated. May your retirement be filled with fulfillment, joy, and the discovery of new possibilities.

I wish you a vibrant and fulfilling retirement journey!

-Subrata Mazumder

Don't miss out!

Visit the website below and you can sign up to receive emails whenever Subrata Mazumder publishes a new book. There's no charge and no obligation.

https://books2read.com/r/B-A-YKHY-PKPJC

BOOKS2READ

Connecting independent readers to independent writers.

About the Author

Subrata Mazumder is an author who seamlessly blends the worlds of engineering and writing. With a background in engineering and a passion for writing, this author has graced the pages of several magazines worldwide, captivating readers with his unique perspectives and engaging storytelling. With a talent for combining technical knowledge with creative flair, he has made a name as a true visionary in both fields. He is retired and lives in Houston with his kids and grandkids.